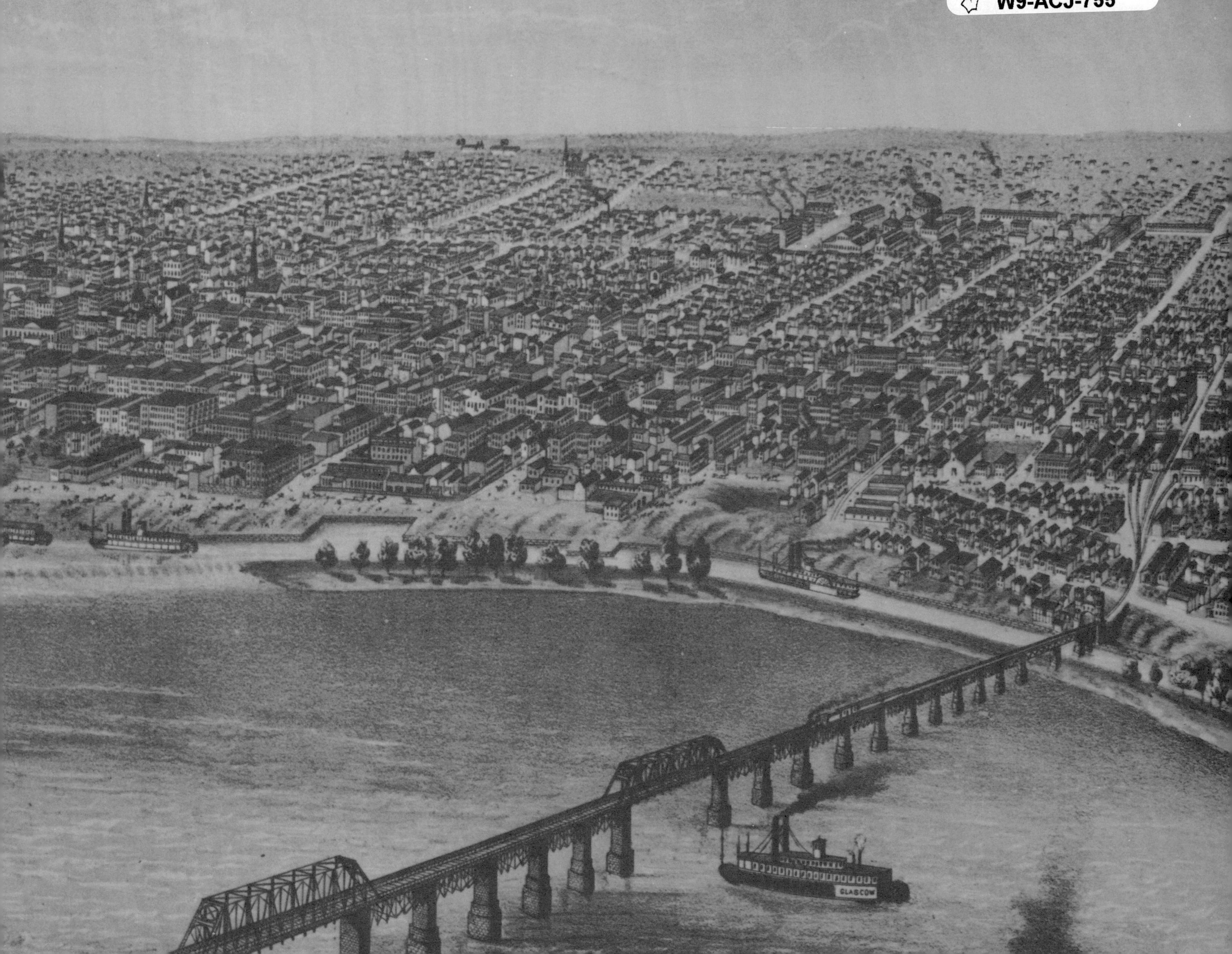
GLASGOW

Old Louisville: The Victorian Era

SECOND & SIXTH

Old Louisville: The Victorian Era

by Samuel W. Thomas
and William Morgan

The Courier-Journal
The Louisville Times
Data Courier, Inc.
1975

3:00 P. M. Central Park 5:00 P. M.

THIS AFTERNOON,

As yesterday's Performance was postponed,

BALDWIN

The Greatest Aeronaut Living, will make his

THRILLING ASCENSION!

CAUTION.—Do not confound this ascension with smoke bags or hot-air fizzles—and one who would maliciously have made a copy of Baldwin's cut, used in yesterday's paper, which did not represent their ascension—as BALDWIN'S leap with the parachute is made from the side of his balloon, while others descend from under, not making a jump. Remember Baldwin uses gas.

DUKE SCHROER,
M'g'r world's leading Aeronauts, the Baldwins.

3 P.M. GRAND CONCERT 3 P.M.

LIBERATI'S

GREAT BAND!

Admission 25c. Children 10c.

FIREWORKS AMPHITHEATER,

TO-NIGHT.

Last Concert!

LIBERATI'S

GREAT BAND

Executive Editor
Samuel W. Thomas

Editor
Mary Lawrence Young

Book Design
Julius Friedman and Nathan Felde,
Images
Louisville, Kentucky

Published by
Data Courier, Inc.
for
The Courier-Journal
The Louisville Times

620 South Fifth Street,
Louisville, Kentucky 40202

Library of Congress
Catalog Number: 75-30382

Printer: Pinaire Lithographing
Corporation, Inc.
Louisville, Kentucky

First Printing: December 1975

Front endpaper: *Bird's Eye View of Louisville, Kentucky, 1876*, published by Charles Shober & Co., Chicago.
Back endpaper: *Birds-Eye View of Louisville from the River Front and Southern Exposition, 1883*, published by M. P. Levyeau & Co., Louisville.
Frontispiece: Second St. north of Jacob St., *ca.* 1893.

Left: *The Courier-Journal*, 31 August 1888.
Opposite: Bedroom in the Pinckney Green House, 1032 Fourth St., *ca.* 1905.

Contents

Preface

The legacy of Victorian architecture in the historic district known as Old Louisville is so rich and diverse, it continues to invite formal examination. Earlier studies depicted only the surviving structures, which were so numerous the false impression was given that Old Louisville was still intact. That assumption has been cited frequently as a reason for the neighborhood's preservation. However, when Old Louisville is viewed from a historical context, there is a sobering realization that a good portion of the prime residential development which took place during the Victorian period already has been obliterated. The northern part of Old Louisville from Broadway to Oak virtually has been rubbed clean of its domestic architecture. The change has been so gradual it is not easy to comprehend the residential and aesthetic loss without a composite picture of how the area looked. To illustrate the significant architectural examples that have been razed and to emphasize the importance of protecting the remaining residential housing, old photographs, especially of the once scenic northern location, were sought for inclusion in this book. The location of each view is given as simply as possible; houses are identified by the principal families who owned them and by a modern street number if possible.

Issues of *The Courier-Journal* and *The Louisville Times* were examined and pertinent articles were excerpted to give a first hand account in the language of the Victorian era. These contemporary reports helped identify the significant architectural examples and the areas of principal development. For instance, an 1888 *Courier-Journal* stated that the "favorite residence quarter for a number of years" was south of Broadway to Magnolia, and from Brook to Fourth streets. With some allowance for expansion beyond Magnolia after the Southern Exposition, this was considered the extent of exemplary Victorian housing. Recent surveys of Old Louisville have tended to examine a larger area. For convenience, the Urban Renewal and Community Development Agency of Louisville in its *The Renewal of Old Louisville* report (1965) included Broadway south to Eastern Parkway and from the North-South Expressway west to Ninth Street. The same area was studied by Theodore M. Brown and Margaret M. Bridwell in their 1961

Broadway east of Third St., 1897.

Second St. south of Jacob St., *ca.* 1893.

publication *Old Louisville.* The Neighborhood Development Corporation defined a smaller district, terminating at Hill Street. Its 1969 study, entitled *Old Louisville: A Challenge and An Opportunity*, also pointed out that residential housing was practically non-existent north of Oak Street. An inventory of the remaining residential area made in 1974 produced an irregularly shaped plot of some 48 square blocks which was designated as the Old Louisville Preservation District by the Historic Landmarks and Preservation Districts Commission. The district boundaries extend south from Kentucky to four blocks beyond Hill Street at one point and west from Interstate-65 to Seventh Street, and include an estimated 1,750 structures.

To avoid these geographic conflicts, this analysis considers Old Louisville in terms of its development as well as its architecture. The illustrations were assembled to create a visual awareness of an era and a former way of life and an appreciation of a picturesque architectural style that seemingly is now so foreign. As the noted architectural historian from Kentucky, Clay Lancaster, stated in his *Introduction to Victorian Houses: A Treasury of Lesser-Known Examples* (Dover, 1973): "The architectural monstrosities of the Victorian period have been created by twentieth-century ignorance."

The authors wish to acknowledge those who provided assistance: Mrs. Hubbard G. Buckner, Mrs. R. Wells Covington, John C. Norman, Carter Ormsby, George H. Yater, Nancy Adams Drye; Elizabeth F. Jones and Douglas L. Stern of the Historic Landmarks and Preservation Districts Commission; James R. Bentley and Martin F. Schmidt of The Filson Club; John J. Cullinane and Margaret A. Thomas of the Preservation Alliance of Louisville and Jefferson County. Also, they are indebted to James N. Keen for graciously providing his superb photographic essay on Old Louisville architectural details.

Rear of the Ford-Green Mansion at
Second and Broadway with Post Office
on Fourth St. in background, *ca.* 1893.

Introduction

The Bicentennial celebration, unfortunately, will tend only to glorify our nation's past when really more effort should be directed to understanding it. History's value is not merely entertainment and commercialism; rather, its careful analysis and interpretation are the bases for society's future improvement. The importance of the events surrounding 1776 cannot be denied, but the rash of commemorations will place so much emphasis on the Colonial era that the anniversary of a subsequent period far more expressive of the American spirit will be ignored. The Philadelphia Centennial Exposition of 1876 mirrored that expansive attitude by showing off the social and technological achievements of its own day. Louisville's Southern Exposition of 1883 also typified the confidence and drive that permeated America following the Civil War. But now that the centennial of the first Centennial period is being so over-shadowed by the pageantry of the Bicentennial, surely there will be no comprehensive interpretation of perhaps the period that most typifies America—the Victorian era from the end of the Civil War to the beginning of the twentieth century.

Understanding the tenor of the Victorian lifestyle is imperative because of its formative role in the development of our complex society. But to compound the problem our impressions of the period are fraught with misconceptions and prejudices. Visual reminders of it, such as streetscapes, seem ugly or even repulsive to present-day Americans.

As Theodore Brown pointed out some years ago in his architectural survey of Old Louisville:

> Our modern eye and taste are primarily attuned to the beauty of smooth, shiny geometric surfaces; thus many people understandably feel a closer aesthetic affinity to the earlier classical forms of the Greek and Renaissance Revivals than to the later Richardsonian. If, however, we approach this later work with an open mind and, more important, open eye, we will discover some of its inherent beauty.

The imaginative blending of architectural components of variously colored and textured materials excited an

Parade floats turning west onto
Broadway from First St., *ca.* 1893.

Row houses built *ca.* 1870 on the northeast corner of Brook and Breckinridge streets, 1961.

emotional response. This rich diversity accentuated the sense of individualism so prevalent during the Victorian development. The flare for novelty and uniqueness provided the community with a recognizable aesthetic character. Louisville's individuality still is manifested most in its Victorian district where technology has not yet homogenized its peculiar architectural features. Its earliest sections, like those in many cities, were once immediately discernible, distinctive and identifiable, but now they have been inundated by a universal mixture of aluminum, glass, and aggregate. The result is that urban centers here and across the country have begun to take on a uniform appearance. Those quirks that once differentiated and distinguished the old avenues have been obliterated. Their replacements are often spectacular structural achievements. However, with the mobility of large architectural and construction firms, the same tower with slight design modifications can go up in any metropolis. It becomes a landmark only by virtue of its being so completely out of human scale. But the monolithic structure does not provide the community identity found in the distinct architecture which results when local architects work with native craftsmen and use indigenous materials. The blend is no longer possible.

The resulting landmarks, when collectively appreciated, immediately identify the community. The district commonly known as Old Louisville has become the city's townprint. Its legacy in richness of design and building material provides the community with an undisputed individuality and identity. Old Louisville emerged in an era of unprecedented change, growth, and confidence which its architecture reflects and measures.

This book provides a means of discovering the visual richness that has been there all the time. It can only hint at the Victorian spirit of Old Louisville, but perhaps in doing so, it will stimulate further study of such a vital time in Louisville's development.

Jacob east of Second St., *ca*. 1893.

A Time and Place

by Samuel W. Thomas

NEW GOTHAM *The Courier-Journal* headline proudly called its city. The word went out during the last decades of the Victorian period that Louisville, Kentucky was an ideal place to live and work. An Olmsted-designed park system, annual industrial growth, available public utilities, healthful climate, extensive streetcar service, educational and cultural opportunities, and an abundance of charities backed up its mounting national reputation as "a city of beautiful homes." The picturesque effect created by the uniform quality of its architecture was impressive. As *The Courier-Journal* remarked on 19 March 1887, "one finds more pretension and display in the houses of the Northern and Eastern cities of the size of Louisville; but nowhere does one find more comfortable houses, more ready hospitality, more generous living, or a more thorough air of ease, quiet and luxurious comfort than in the dwelling places of Louisville." Yet despite this facade of tranquility, a fundamental transformation was taking place.

The city's character and image of itself changed abruptly during this prosperous segment of the Victorian era. Similar brief but intense bursts of economic development have marked Louisville's past with remarkable degrees of regularity both before and since the late Victorian period. Roughly every 50 years the city has been jolted from complacency by significant surges of commercial growth, technological advancement and residential expansion.

The initial boom took place in the early 1780s following the Revolutionary War and was marked by extensive pioneer settlement. The second development period occurred in the early 1830s and witnessed, with the completion of the Louisville and Portland Canal, the emergence of the city as a potent western commercial force. One hundred years later, echoing the gaiety of a nation caught in the mood of the Roaring Twenties, Louisville experienced its fourth wave of growth as Fourth Street anchored a thriving district for entertainment, retail sales and professional services. The fifth and current age of expansion is perhaps best symbolized by the Chamber of Commerce slogan "City of the Seventies." Major office struc-

Left: Queen Anne stairway, 1436 Third St., 1961. Above: Houses on the northwest corner of Fourth and Park Avenue presently owned by the Woman's Club of Louisville, 1897.

tures and public open spaces have been constructed, and a new concept of "downtown" is evolving.

But in Louisville's evolutionary process, the third boom period was certainly the longest, and strongest, and the most significant. During the late 1870s and early 1880s, the city became engaged in the industrial thrust that characterized the latter part of the Victorian age.

A dormant southern town before the Civil War, Louisville capitalized on its position as a rail and river transportation center to become a robust community with developing manufacturing and cultural interests. The economic confidence rekindled nationally during the early post-War years and locally by spanning the Ohio River for the first time by a railroad bridge in 1870, resulted in unparalleled increases in both industrial and public construction which reached their peak in the late 1880s. The era marked Louisville's conversion to a diverse manufacturing community. In doing so, a sizeable proprietary and managerial class was produced, and for the first time a neighborhood emerged that was composed of residents brought together by similar social and economic interests, not by religious and ethnic considerations. Old Louisville exists as the picturesque legacy of that dynamic moment of change and expansion.

The prime location for residential development during the peak years prior to 1890 and shortly thereafter was only a part of what is now considered Old Louisville. Residential construction was confined generally to an area bounded north and south by Broadway and Hill Street and east and west by Brook and Sixth streets. *The Courier-Journal* of 6 September 1888 noted:

> The favorite residence quarter for a number of years was south from Broadway, which divides the city parallel with the river. South Fourth, Third, Second, First, and Brook streets, are lined with lovely and costly houses in which the taste of the architect and the landscape gardener vie with each other for expression. Magnolia Avenue, Kentucky, Oak, and St. Catherine streets, which intersect the others at right

Member of the Louisville Cycle Club, *ca.* 1890.

Opposite: Oakland Race Course painted by Robert Brammer, 1840. Site near Seventh and Magnolia streets was a stable during the Civil War.

OAKLAND
HOUSE

Second St. south from Broadway, *ca.* 1893.

angles, are within this charming district, and present the same lovely spectacle.

Unfortunately, most of the domestic architecture in the northern section of Old Louisville, especially between Broadway and Kentucky Street, has been eliminated by surface parking, an expressway, and an expanding commercial core. The loss of this section of the neighborhood has had detrimental effects on retail business in the downtown area. This should come as no surprise because retail development has followed residential movement ever since the first settlers began moving their homes away from the waterfront. The outer reaches of house construction always established the city limits. For logistical reasons, the wholesalers and distributors hovered around the wharf area, principally on Main Street. The retailers were in between, and as the residents moved further south and the retailers followed, the first residential streets were enveloped.

The earliest homes were located along Jefferson and Walnut, and later Chestnut Street. Domestic construction south of Jefferson Street was evidently too sparse to delineate on the first city map (J. Flint, 1824) that showed the location and outline of structures. The city surveyor's plan, published in 1831 and reduced for the first city directory in 1832, indicated that the established city blocks had been divided into eight and 10 lots each, but that the land between Liberty and Prather streets remained in five-, 10-, and 20-acre "ranges." Only Preston, Fifth, and Seventh streets extended beyond the town line along Prather Street, now Broadway.

An accurate bird's eye view *(p. 22)* published by Charles Magnus of New York about 1855 depicted little development south of Broadway except out First Street even though the second map to be published in a city directory (1856) showed an extensive criss-cross street pattern beyond Broadway. At that time, most thoroughfares terminated at Kentucky Street, the revised (1836) incorporation boundary. Both the Bergmann map of Jefferson County (1858) *(p. 23)* and the U.S. Engineers' Civil War defenses map of 1865 *(p. 23)* confirm that development south of Kentucky Street did

Sidewalk decoration at 1393 Second St., 1961.

Above: The Johnston-Woolley House, built *ca.* 1848 on the north side of Jefferson between Brook and Floyd streets, was a rare example of Greek Revival in Louisville's domestic architecture. *The Courier-Journal*, 6 September 1888. Demolished. Right: The George Douglass Sherley residence with Italianate features and Greek Revival decoration was erected *ca.* 1842 on the southwest corner of Third and Chestnut streets. Shown about 1890, it became the site of the Henry Clay Hotel.

Left: C. P. Moorman's *ca.* 1872 Italian villa on the west side of Fourth St. between Chestnut and Broadway, shown in 1918. Above: Southeast corner of Seventh and Chestnut streets, *The Courier-Journal*, 6 September 1888. Houses from right to left were owned by: B. W. Wood, W. A. Davis, and Dennis Long.

Louisville, Ky., published by Charles Magnus, New York, *ca*. 1855. Beargrass Creek then entered the Ohio River between Third and Fourth streets.

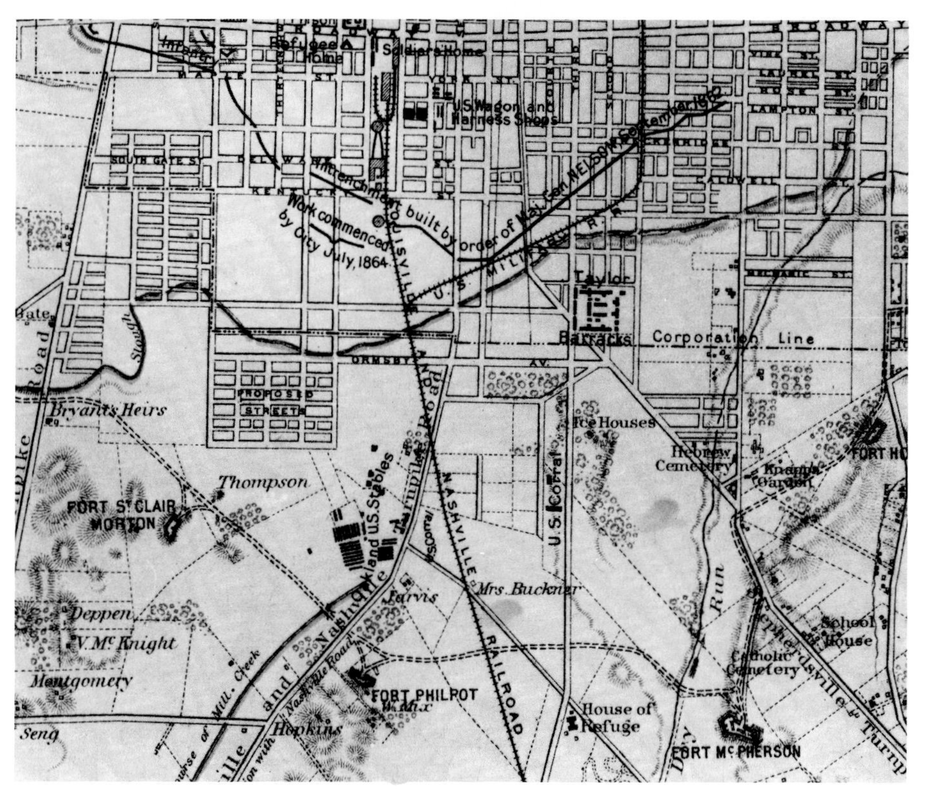

Above: *Map of Jefferson County, Kentucky*, published by G. T. Bergmann, surveyor, 1858. Below: *Louisville and Its Defenses*, by U.S. Engineers, 1864-1865.

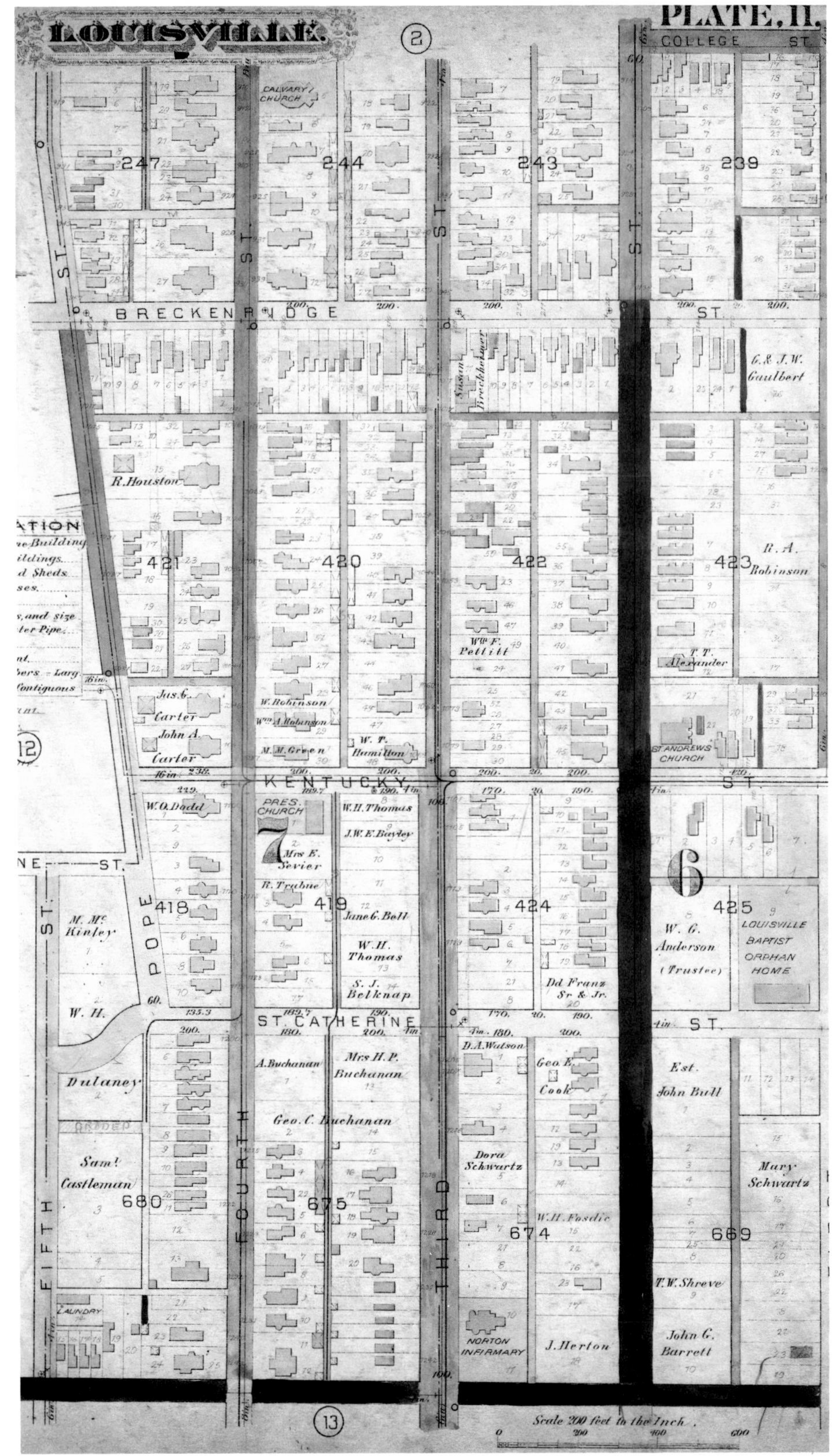

Atlas of the City of Louisville, Ky., 1884.

not occur until later. During the War a sizeable Union installation known as Taylor Barracks occupied the two-block-square area between First and Third north of Ormsby.

The first atlas of Louisville, published in 1876, not only delineated houses of substantial proportions along Broadway but also out the cross streets, Second, Third and Fourth, south to Kentucky. This represents an important change in the way the city was expanding. For the first time, the flow of development was concentrated along a north-south axis. Since the founding of the town, the principal streets had been east-west thoroughfares parallel to the river, used predominantly for single purposes such as commerce, retailing or residence. The cross streets had been mere dividers. During the Victorian period, Fourth Street became a unified but multipurpose artery and its length was a microcosm of the city. At its northern end was the bustling retail district. Concentrated between Liberty and Broadway were churches, an exhibition hall, public library, and hospital. Mule cars ran in and out from the fashionable residential area south of Broadway. Uptown and downtown had referred to the east and west of center city, but when Fourth Street assumed added importance, they became north-south designations.

When the next atlas appeared in 1884, the corridor of exclusive residences on either side of Third and Fourth streets had extended three blocks further to Ormsby Street (*pp. 24, 26*). Very little construction had taken place south of Ormsby, although the land, including the House of Refuge property (which would become the University of Louisville campus), had been incorporated into the city limits in 1868, and streets had been laid out and marked off. The vacant lots in this portion of Old Louisville were readily available for the building explosion that occurred between the beginning of the Southern Exposition in 1883 and the devastating tornado of 1890.

Placing the Southern Exposition on the present site of St. James and Belgravia courts riveted both local and national attention on Old Louisville's attributes and hastened its development. As *The Courier-Journal* (*p. 110*) exclaimed in banner headlines on 2 August 1883: "THE GREAT SOUTHERN

Above: Fourth St. north from Broadway, *ca.* 1890. St. Aloysius College (*ca.* 1850) later the site of St. Joseph's Infirmary at right. Right: Central Park mule car heading out Fourth St. about 1875.

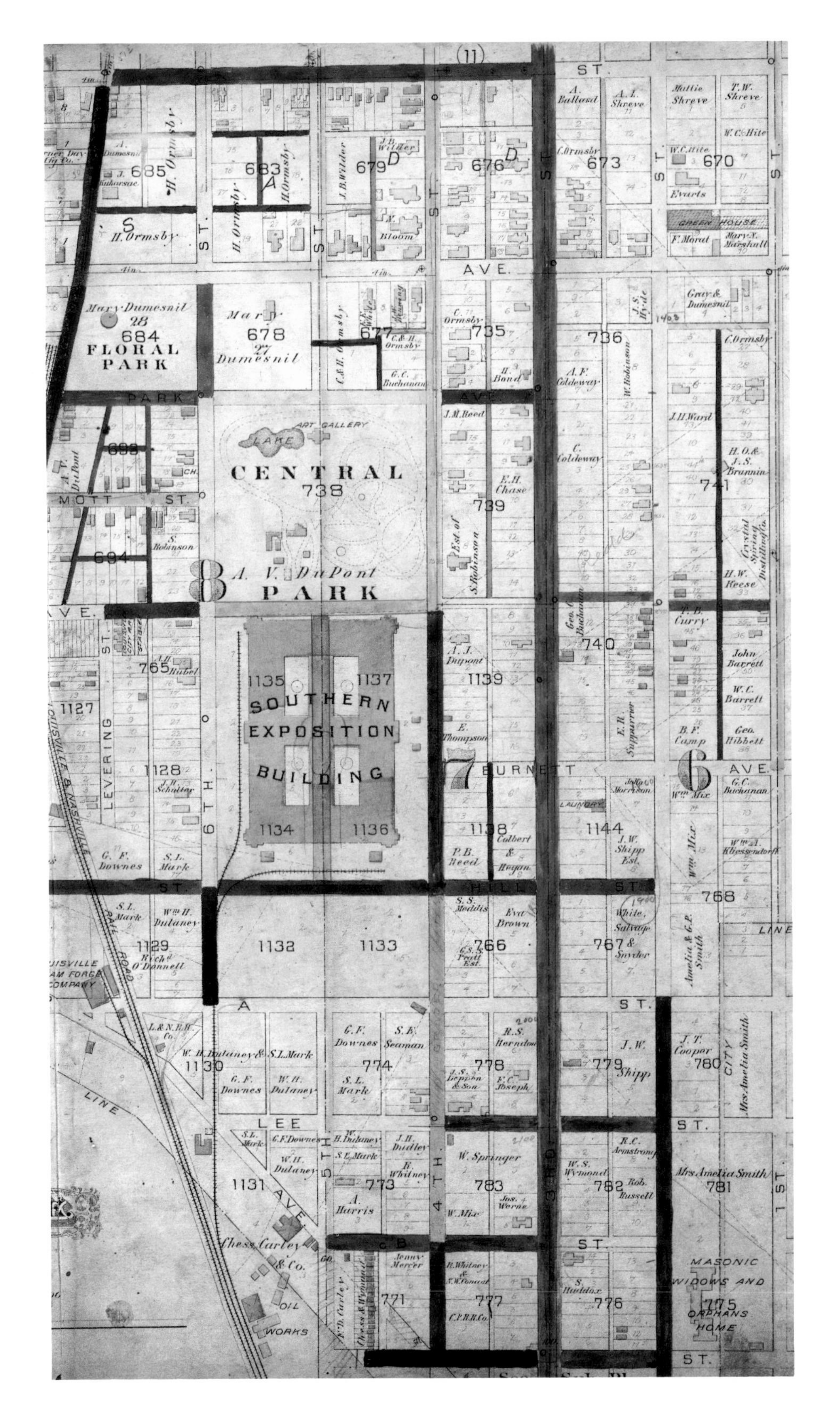

Atlas of the City of Louisville, Ky.,
1884.

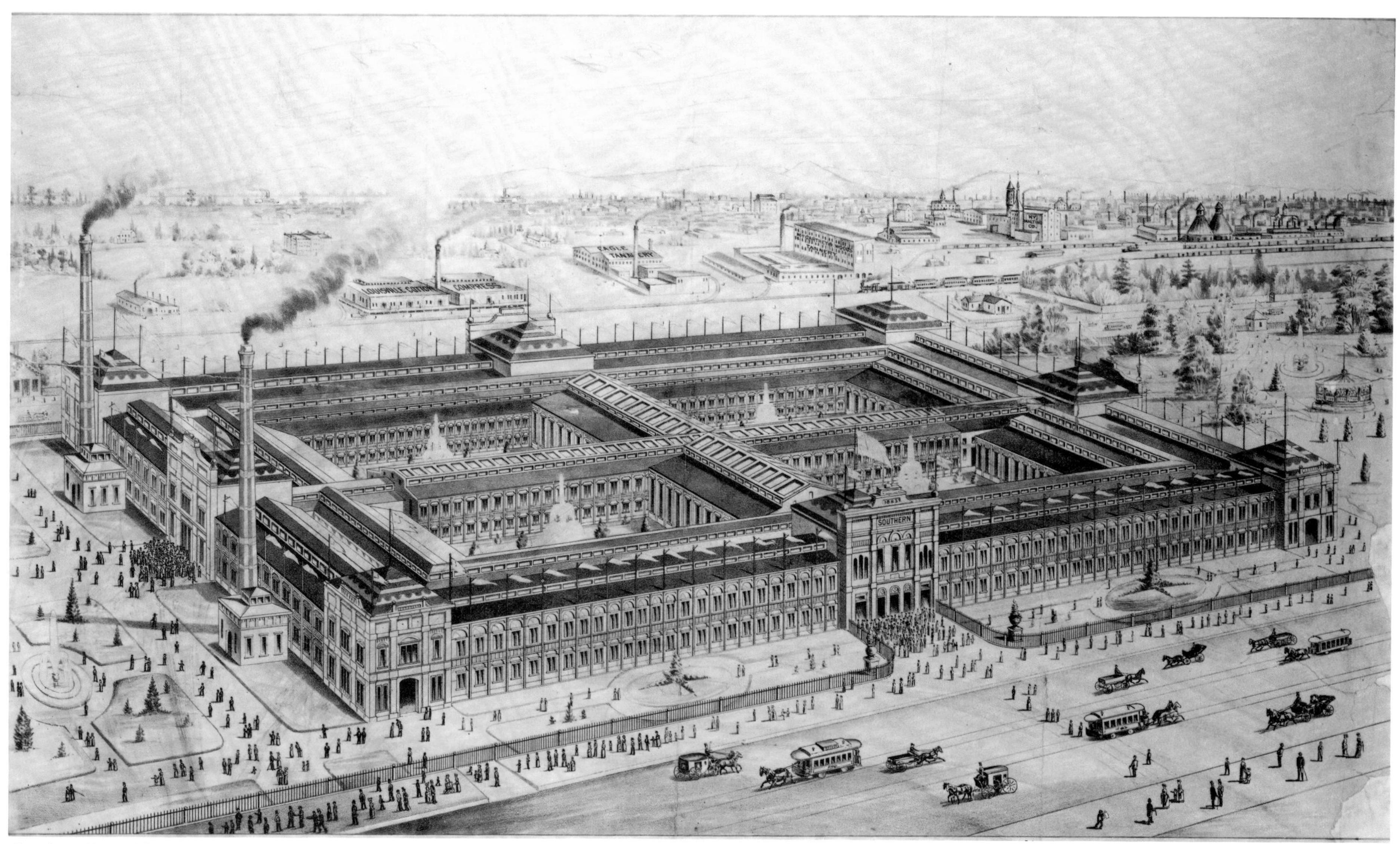

Southern Exposition and industry west
of Sixth St., 1883.

EXPOSITION THROWS ITS DOORS OPEN TO THE WORLD." Before it closed in 1887, the Exposition attracted several million visitors, stimulating the formation of an extensive streetcar transportation system (*p. 87*) that helped open the southern quarter of the city.

Expositions on a much smaller scale had been demonstrating the "mechanical arts" and industrial output of Louisville off and on for 30 years. The Kentucky Mechanics Institute moved its exhibit hall (*p. 29*) to the northeast corner of Fourth and Broadway six years prior to being disbanded because of the Civil War. The Louisville Industrial Exposition re-established the practice by building an impressive brick hall (*p. 28*) at Fourth and Chestnut streets in 1872. It too had a rather speedy demise as the property was sold to the federal government in 1883 to make way for the site of the Post Office (*p. 90*).

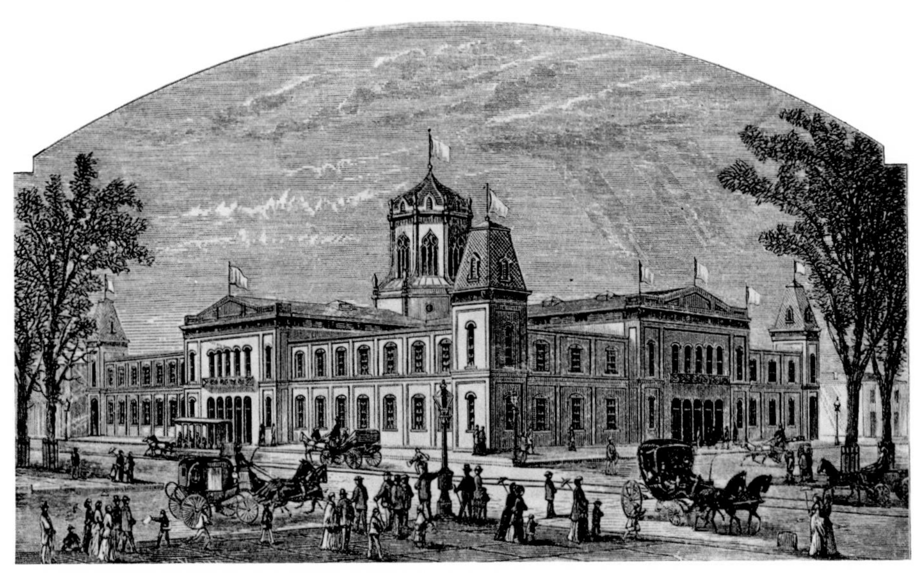

Louisville Industrial Exposition opened on the northeast corner of Fourth and Chestnut streets in 1872.

"The idea of holding at Louisville an Exposition international in spirit but Southern in enterprise" was first broached by a *Courier-Journal* editorial in 1880. But when Louisville did not move rapidly on the proposal, Atlanta did, and it "has made a city of her, while Louisville has lost, for the time being, an opportunity to establish herself as the city of the South."

In the issue marking the Exposition's opening *The Courier-Journal* reiterated its initial stance:

> that there should be given in the South an exhibition of all her resources, agricultural, mineral, and mechanical, of which cotton should be the principal feature, because it was peculiarly a Southern product and a staple of the South. The Atlanta Cotton Exposition, while a most extensive affair, and of its kind a great success, did not comprehend this idea in its results, and it was the opinion of the papers that there remained to Louisville the opportunity to perfect the good work begun by her sister city.

Finally in late 1882, the concept was accepted and plans were formulated and executed by a "Committee of Fifty" influential citizens. When the Southern Exposition opened, the inaugural ceremony (*p. 111*) was preceded by a procession

Stancliff and Vodges were the architects for the Kentucky Mechanics Institute's Exhibition Building, lithographed by Robyn & Co., Louisville, in 1854.

from the Galt House through the city and out Fourth Street to the Exposition grounds. Buildings along the way were gaily decorated with a "profusion of flags, bunting, Chinese lanterns, evergreen wreaths, arches, pictures and festoons that was almost Oriental in its magnificence." Following remarks by the mayor and governor, President Chester Arthur pulled a rope to set in motion the exhibition's machinery, symbolizing America's newly achieved supremacy in the industrial world.

The various exhibit structures and floral gardens spread over nearly 50 acres, surrounding the main exposition hall (*p. 27*) that was perhaps the largest wooden structure of its kind ever erected. Only the London Exposition's Crystal Palace and the Philadelphia Centennial's Main Building encompassed more than the Southern Exposition hall's 13 acres. It is difficult to imagine a hall of such vast proportions as 600 by 900 feet, but it is even more difficult to comprehend that such an immense edifice would house mechanical, manufactured, and cultural exhibits for only five years and then be dismantled. Local architects McDonald Brothers & Curtain designed a series of pivotal windows and continuous skylights for adequate ventilation and natural light. Installation of 4,600 16-candle lamps supervised by their inventor, Thomas Edison himself, made this exposition the first that could be viewed at night. Even the grounds, which included DuPont Square (now Central Park) were illuminated by another new source of light—arc lamps.

The Satellites of Mercury formed their parades at Sixth and Hill streets and proceeded along a circuitous route through the city. An estimated 200,000 people watched their 21 floats in 1889. *The Courier-Journal*, 5 October 1889.

Opposite: The Henry A. Dumesnil residence on the south side of Ormsby between Fifth and Sixth streets. The last section of the house was added about 1868. Photographed *ca.* 1885, it is the site of the Adams House.

The extravaganza fulfilled its expectations and provided quite a psychological boost to the citizenry. But after several highly successful years marked by many cultural and amusement highlights, the Exposition became merely an outlet for display of manufactured goods. Ultimately it ceased to attract sufficient visitors.

Nearby parks and amusement centers, however, continued to flourish and generate interest in Old Louisville. Floral Park's rows of rare and ornamental shrubs and flowers were maintained by the Dumesnil family in the entire block diagonally northwest across Sixth Street from DuPont Square. The Fireworks Ampitheater (*p. 33*) that could seat 10,000 people was located south of Hill Street, between Fourth and Fifth

Opposite: Louisville Athletic Club constructed in 1889 at Zane and Garvin Place. Shown about 1892, this superb Queen Anne structure has been demolished.

Above. The Fireworks Amphitheater on the west side of Fourth St. between Hill and Gaulbert could seat 10,000 people for pyrotechnic displays when it opened in 1890. Left: The Amphitheater Auditorium at the southwest corner of Fourth and Hill streets opened in 1889.

Section of the Robinson-DuPont House in Central Park added *ca.* 1868. House was razed in 1904. Interior photographs on this and the opposite page were made *ca.* 1890.

streets. It was adjacent to the Auditorium (*p. 33*) on the southwest corner of Fourth and Hill streets. The Louisville Tennis Club (*p. 134*) was also on Fourth. The facilities of the Louisville Athletic Club (*p. 32*) were at Zane and Garvin Place. The principal attraction in Old Louisville even before and certainly after the Southern Exposition was DuPont Square's forest setting.

A. V. DuPont had purchased the bucolic, 18-acre site (*pp. 114, 144*) and brick house (*pp. 34, 35*) from Stuart Robinson in 1871. He continued to permit public access to view the trees and flower beds on the property and later allowed the Southern Exposition to build the Art Museum and lake (*p. 115*) near Park Avenue. DuPont even agreed at that time to sell the property to the city for Central Park but it was not purchased until 1904. Then, the DuPont House, the Art Museum, and other outbuildings were removed and the grounds were laid out formally by the Olmsted firm of Boston.

The adjacent site of the Southern Exposition was cleared and subdivided into residential lots (*p. 36*) known as St. James Court in 1890. It sparked the most frenzied land speculation and building boom in the city's history. The bonanza had been growing for several years. *The Courier-Journal* reported that in 1885, 260 residences had been built south of Broadway at an average cost of $6,150. The city *Directory* commented that twice as many brick buildings were erected in 1887 as in 1886. And the *Directory* of 1888 stated that the "prospect was never better for any year than it is for 1889 in the line of building operations . . . and it is safe to say that the exhibit for 1889 will eclipse that of any former year in the city's history. In the matter of homes, Louisville justly stands pre-eminent among all as the 'residence city of America.' "

Such progress is borne out by increased population figures. The *Louisville Directory* of 1888 explained that an "increase of population means *work* for the merchants, the manufacturer, the builder, the artisan, the laborer and the professions—it further means an expanding commerce, a demand for and consequent growth of all the varied industries that make up 'the hum' of a wide awake, progressive city." The popula-

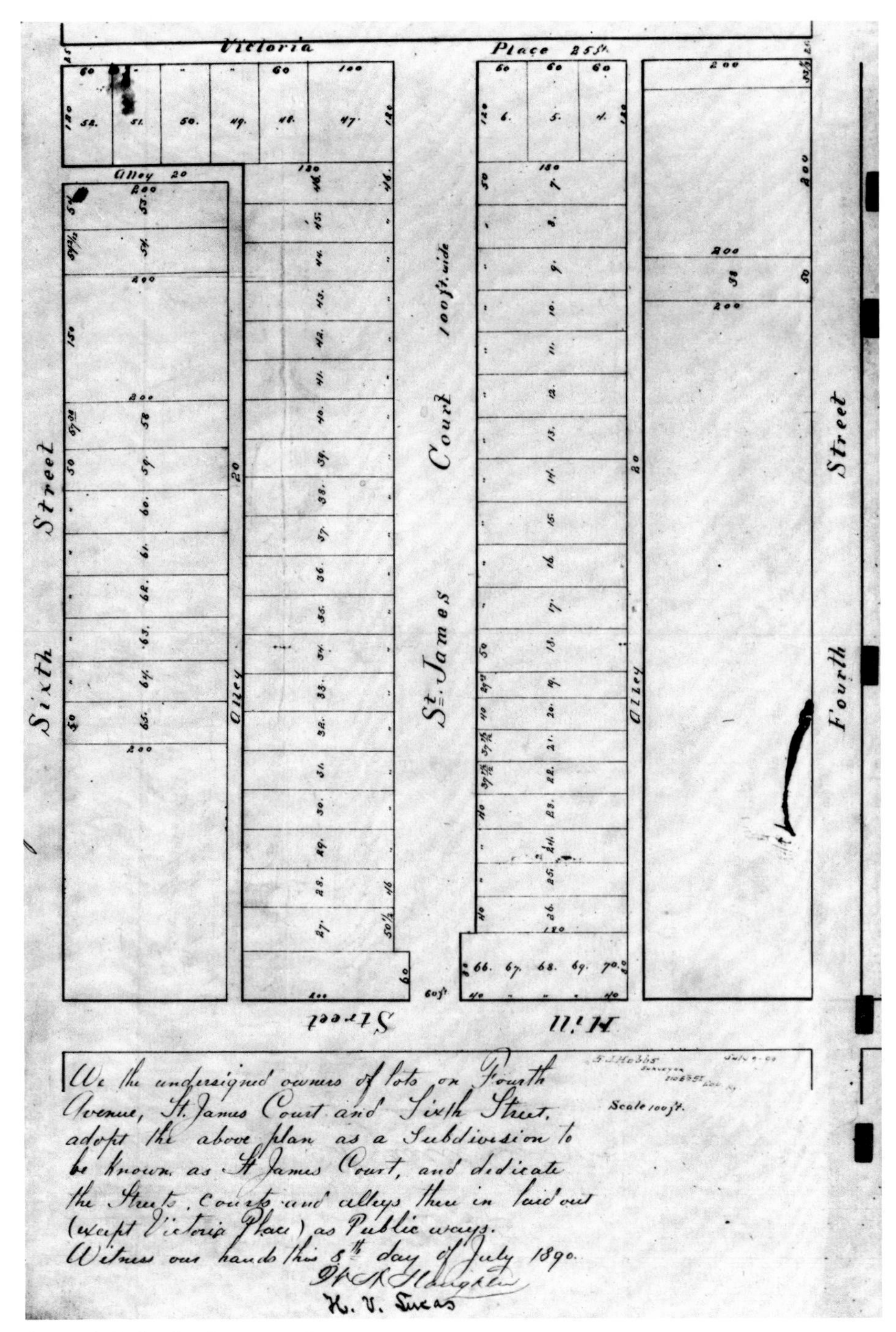

Amended plat for St. James Court, 23 August 1890. Belgravia Court had not been planned. Jefferson County Deed Book 357, p. 638.

Left: Entrance to Central Park from St. James Court, *ca.* 1892. Below: West side of St. James Court in 1897.

Railroad yard near Tenth and
Maple streets, *ca.* 1893.

Opposite: Third St. north of Park
Avenue, 1897.

Top: Cherokee Rd. east toward Grinstead Drive, 1903. Bottom: Third St. looking north toward Confederate Monument, 1903.

Top: Third St., east side between Lee and Bloom streets, 1903. Bottom: Third St. looking north from Gaulbert, 1903.

tion of Louisville had at least doubled in every decade between 1790 and 1850. The rate of increase then began to diminish significantly but continued to average 50 per cent in the decades between 1850 and 1880. The population exceeded 100,000 for the first time in 1870 and the federal census of 1880 recorded 123,762 persons. Within the federal census periods, population figures were projected by commercial and civic interest groups and provided for the city directories. The city populace numbered 177,950 in 1888, a 44 per cent increase from 1880. The yearly increase from 1880 through 1888 had averaged 6,340 persons, and in 1887 alone, more than 10,700 new inhabitants were living in Louisville. As the *Directory* remarked, "these figures are gratifying and astonishing, and for a staid and conservative city, a little bit phenomenal."

The *Directory* (1889) also correlated the influence of population growth with changes in housing.

> During 1888 there were 934 new buildings erected in this city. For the few years prior to 1888 there were many new enterprises begun in Louisville, and many artisans and mechanics came to make their homes here. This created a demand for residences, and the large proportion of the buildings of 1888 being frame is thus explained. The fact that, while the number of buildings for 1888 is greater than for 1887, the cost of their construction is $225,530 less, is also explained. The demand for modest dwellings, such as would give the mechanic a home to himself at a cheap rental, was evidenced last year by the buildings operations. The new homes show of what order of men Louisville's increase in population is mostly composed. The additions to her houses and population show that the incomers are of that class which produce the wealth and importance of a city—the brawn and muscle of the land.

The growth figures and favorable economic climate prompted national recognition. For the first time Louisville received equal press billing with Cincinnati, long considered its

TRUSTEE'S SALE.

TRUSTEE'S SALE

$50,000 worth of valuable improved Real Estate and other property must be sold, regardless of cost, at whatever it will bring, to wind up a trust. The best opportunity ever offered in the city for investments and bargains.

As Trustee, I offer for sale, to suit purchasers, until May 1, the following described real and personal property:

First—The real estate and buildings known as the Long & Bro. Manufacturing Company's factory. This property is situated on the southwest corner of Washington and Webster streets, consisting of a lot of ground 150 feet front on Washington street, extending back on Webster street 150 feet to a paved alley. All streets and sidewalks made, with public cistern and well at corner of the two streets. The buildings consist of a large three-story, metal-roof brick, with cellar 50 feet by 100 feet; two-story brick dry-room; one-story brick boiler-house; two-story frame, metal-roof machine building; one-story frame, metal-roof work-shop; two-story corrugated iron machine and work-shops; two steam dry rooms; one blacksmith shop. The ground and above-mentioned buildings cost over twenty-five thousand dollars, and are well adapted to most any kind of manufacturing business, work-shops or warehouse, and well located. I will sell the above property as a whole on the most favorable terms—part cash, balance on long payments with lien retained at 6 per cent. interest. This property offers the best opportunity ever presented in this city for a great bargain, and must be sold for what it will bring.

Second—I also offer for sale, separate and distinct from the above property, in lots to suit purchasers, for cash, the following list of property, to-wit: Two splendid boilers; one large boiler heater; two horizontal engines, nearly as good as new; 450 feet of main and counter shafting; a large number of shafting hangers and collars; 300 pulleys of desirable sizes; about 100 machines of all kinds for wood-work, suited for chairs, furniture, etc., such as cut-off, rip, band and jig saws; planers, moulders, hand and gauge lathes; one iron tool lathe; one iron drilling machine, boring machines, mortising machines, friezers, matchers, dressers, sandpapering and polishing machines, etc.; 2,600 feet of good leather belting, from 2 inches in width up to 14 inches; 4,890 feet of steam pipe, from ½ inch up to 2 inches; about 100,000 pounds of wrought and cast-iron castings, clasps and hoop iron; cabinet and other work benches, blacksmith tools and forge; large lot of screws, files, knives, bits and other tools; office safe, desks, chairs, etc.

All of this list of personal property will be sold for whatever it will bring, notwithstanding its original cost was over twenty-five thousand dollars, and now is the opportunity to get such articles regardless of cost or value; as all of the property herein described will be peremptorily sold to wind up the affairs of my trust.

If not disposed of in whole or in part, I will, on the premises, May 1, between the hours of 10 o'clock a. m. and 5 o'clock p. m., and so on from day to day until sold, sell said property, or whatever may be unsold, at public sale to the highest bidder. Apply to R. C. Kerr, real estate agent, No. 289 Fifth street, between Main and Market, who will show the property and act as my agent in the premises, or apply to the undersigned.

H. C. RODES, Trustee,
Citizens' National Bank, cor. Main and Bullitt sts.

FUTURE AUCTION SALES.

AT AUCTION

By C. C. Nalley & Co.

Monday Morning at 10 O'clock

CARPETS, Bed-room Suits, Wardrobes, Stoves, Parlor, Dining-room and Kitchen Furniture at a sacrifice.

Terms cash.

C. C. NALLY & CO.,
Furniture, Storage and Commission Merchants, 323 W. Market st.

By Gus F. Rothenburger.

BUILDING LOTS ON WEST BROADWAY AND WALNUT STS.—4 handsome building lots on south side of Broadway, between Twenty-fourth and Twenty-fifth sts., each lot fronts 30 feet by a depth of 180 feet to an alley. Also one lot, on the south side of Walnut, bet. Twenty-seventh and Twenty-eighth streets. The only lot left on the south side.

AT AUCTION,

On Monday afternoon, April 22, at 4:30 o'clock, on the premises, I will sell the above named lots on Broadway; said lots lie nice and high, streets and sidewalks made. This neighborhood is building up fast. These lots will surely enhance in value. And on the same day, at 5 o'clock, I will sell the Walnut-st. lot above named. Terms—One-third cash, balance 1 and 2 years, 6 per cent. interest and lien.

AUCTION SALE OF BOOTS AND SHOES BY *F. G. SNYDER & CO., 230 6th ST.,* Monday, April 22, '89, COMMENCING AT 10 O'CLOCK PROMPT!

STORAGE OF HOUSEHOLD EFFECTS,

REAL ESTATE.

WESTVIEW BUILDING COMP'Y

Handsome SUBURBAN RESIDENCES for sale on PARKLAND HILLS. STOP paying RENT for NOTHING and BUY a HOME with the money.

CHOICE Investment AND Building Lots For Sale on Easy Terms.

Street Cars EVERY Fifteen Minutes. Daisy Trains EVERY Forty Minutes.

Parkland Hills is Louisville's Most Desirable Suburb.

WESTVIEW BUILDING CO.

435 Jefferson St., bet. 4th and 5th, Louisville, Ky.

Branch Office—Cor. Olive and Dumesnil Streets, Parkland.

Geo. M. Crawford. Secretary.

AT PRIVATE SALE.

Finest Location on Silver Hills,

EDGE HILL PLACE,

Located one mile northwest of New Albany, Ind., on Paoli pike. The magnificent summer residence of the late Judge S. K. Wolfe is now for sale. This splendid property is finely located on Silver Hills, 400 feet above the Ohio river, overlooking all the falls cities, and consisting of 75 acres of excellent land, a fine two-story brick residence of eleven rooms and three-story observatory, with all modern conveniences, good barn and all outbuildings in first-class condition, all having been built in the past six years; also two fine orchards of choice fruit trees and one large vineyard, besides small fruits in great abundance of every known variety. For shade, water, fruits, and the comforts of a rural home this place can not be excelled. There is on the place a good tenant house. Also another hill place of seven acres, within one mile from city, for sale; good view and shade.

For particulars address EDW. W. WOLFE, New Albany, Ind.

FUTURE AUCTION SALES.

By Meddis, Southwick & Co.

HANDSOME HOUSEHOLD FURNITURE.

Latest Styles, Elegantly Finished, Nearly New,

AT AUCTION,

WE will sell at the above residence the choicest assortment of household furniture offered this season, consisting of latest style of Parlor Furniture, in Satin Brocatelle, assorted colors; Antique Oak Dining-Room Furniture, very handsome, with embossed leather seated chairs; Walnut, Mahogany and Antique Oak Chamber Suits; Body Brussels Carpets throughout; Haviland Chinaware; Glassware, etc.; Bric-a-Brac, etc.; Hall Heating Stove, tile finished. This is certainly a rare assortment of furniture, and merits the attention of housekeepers and those contemplating housekeeping.

Terms cash.

MEDDIS, SOUTHWICK & CO

BY MEDDIS, SOUTHWICK & CO

ASSIGNEE SALE.

Lots Nos. 11 and 24 in Castleman's Breckinridge-street Addition

AT AUCTION.

MONDAY MORNING, APRIL 22, 1889,

about the hour of 12 o'clock, at the Court House door, immediately after the Marshal's Sale, I will sell, as assignee of E. M. Pierce, two lots south side Breckinridge street in the above addition, to the highest bidder.

Terms—One-third cash, balance one and two years, 6 per cent. interest, and lien notes negotiable and payable in bank.

RANDOLPH H. BLAINE, Assignee.

MEDDIS, SOUTHWICK & CO., Auctioneers.

By Meglemry & Brandeis.

AT AUCTION.

FUTURE AUCTION SALES

Large and Important Auction Sales

By THOS. ANDERSON & CO.

Commencing Tuesday, April 23, at 10 a. m., with an Extra Large and Desirable Stock of BOOTS AND SHOES, direct from the Manufacturers, in almost every style and quality of Seasonable Goods; also the stock of a city retailer declining business.

WEDNESDAY, April 24, an assorted stock of Dry Goods, Notions, Carpets, Oil Cloths, Silk Parasols, Embroideries, Straw Hats, etc., etc.

THURSDAY, April 25, important sale of CLOTHING, by order of New York, Cincinnati, Baltimore and other manufacturers, comprising Men's, Youths', Boys' and Children's Suits in great variety; Pants, Summer Coats and Vests; also retail stock of Clothing; also Fur, Wool and Straw Hats, Men's Mackinaw Hats and Gents' Furnishing Goods. Terms cash.

J. L. BRENT, Auctioneer.

By BUCHANAN & BRO.

Executor's Auction Sale of 2½-story Brick Dwelling of 12 rooms, No. 627, east side Seventh street, north of Walnut.

TUESDAY AFTERNOON at 5 o'clock, April 23, 1889, on the premises, by the authority vested in me as executor of Nannie P. Peak, deceased, I will sell at public auction, the above described dwelling, with lot fronting 23 feet 10 inches by 204 feet to an alley.

Terms—One-third cash, remainder in one and two years, notes negotiable and payable in bank, with 6 per cent. interest, secured by a lien.

J. J. BROWN,
Executor of Nannie P. Peak.
By BUCHANAN & BRO., His Agents.

ASSIGNEE'S SALE

—AT AUCTION.—

AS Assignee of the Branham Printing Co., I will on FRIDAY, APRIL 26, 1889, at 11 o'clock a. m., on the premises, No. 1018 West Market street, between Tenth and Eleventh streets, in this city, offer for sale the entire outfit and machinery of the said Printing Company, consisting in part of a large lot of type of the best kinds, one Campbell Country Press and Attachments, one Peerless Press, one Gordon Press, one Six Horse Power Engine, Boiler, etc., one Economy Paper Cutter, one large Detroit Safe, Office Fixtures, etc. In short, everything connected with a first-class printing establishment. All free of incumbrance. TERMS AT SALE.

W. A. MERIWETHER, Auctioneer. H. S. IRWIN, Assignee, Etc.

Administratrix's Sale.

EXECUTOR'S SALE

Of one of the Most Valuable Main Street Stores,

No. 334 S. S. Main, bet. Third and Fourth,

Now Leased for $1,400 Per Year,

AT AUCTION,

Monday, April 29, at 5 o'clock P.M

By order of the FIDELITY TRUST COMPANY, executor of Elenor E. Starkey, deceased, we will, on the day and date above, sell, on the premises, that magnificent three-story stone front store-house now occupied by C. P. Hess & Co. and leased to them and W. H. McKnight for three years at $1,400 per year. This is a substantially-built house, splendidly located and a magnificent investment. Lot 17 4-12 by 210.

Terms—One-fourth cash, balance one, two and three years, six per cent. semi-annually.

MEDDIS, SOUTHWICK & CO., Auctioneers.

BY MEDDIS, SOUTHWICK & CO.

ADMINISTRATOR'S SALE!

—OF—

One of the Handsomest Private Residences

IN THIS CITY,

The Palatial Stone-Front Residence of the late Isaac Wolf, deceased,

S. E. COR. FLOYD AND BROADWAY,

AT AUCTION.

By order of Fidelity Trust Co., Administrator with will annexed, we will sell to the highest bidder on the premises, this magnificent residence and grounds on

Tuesday, April 23, 1889, at 4 P. M.

This entire establishment is almost without an equal in its appointments, surroundings and advantages. Unlimited means was expended in its construction. It is provided with every devise and convenience conducive to comfort and luxury. Its location is now unsurpassed, and when Broadway is reconstructed on the plan proposed by His Honor, Mayor Jacob, it will be the grandest boulevard in the south or west, and all other residence streets will pale into insignificence when compared with it.

This house with carriage house, servants' house and all its appointments from cellar to roof is first-class in design, workmanship and material, and is in as perfect and thorough order as the day it was completed.

It can be seen any time prior to sale by application to the undersigned. Lot, 105x200 to alley. Terms at sale.

MEDDIS, SOUTHWICK & CO.,
For FIDELITY TRUST CO., Adm'r with will annexed.

BY HALE & BRO.

—AND—

MEDDIS, SOUTHWICK & CO.

Manufacturing Lots! Manufacturing Lots!

On the Short-line Connection Railroad and Floyd Street, Between D and G Streets.

1,170x125 feet deep, fronting immediately on the above railroad connection on the east side and running back towards Floyd street, embracing 89 lots of 30 feet each.

540x125 feet fronting the west side of Floyd street, extending back towards the above railroad property, which could be purchased and used in connection with the above if desired.

AT AUCTION

TUESDAY AFTERNOON, MAY 7, AT 4 O'CLOCK,

We will sell on the premises, on the Short-line Connection Railroad, between D and G streets, just east of the House of Refuge, some of the most valuable manufacturing property around the city. This locality already has the Kentucky Wagon Works Co., the Louisville Chair Factory and the T. H. Meehan Cooperage Works, all of which are new enterprises in this locality—a strong indorsement of its advantages for manufacturing purposes. This property should be looked after by manufacturers. If you don't want it now, YOU WILL WANT IT, and now is the time to buy. For speculation it is attractive.

TERMS—One-fourth cash, balance 1, 2 and 3 years, 6 per cent. interest and lien notes negotiable and payable in bank.

HALE & BROTHER,
MEDDIS, SOUTHWICK & CO., Auctioneers.

BY HEINSHEIMER & JOSEPH.

$10,000!

Contents of I. T. Cusack's Mammoth Chinaware house, No. 1082 W. Market st., bet. Tenth and Eleventh, consisting of elegant Dinner and Tea Sets, all kinds of Glassware, splendid Vases, Handsome Bric-a-Brac, Cutlery of all kinds, Plated Ware, in fact everything carried in a first-class establishment.

The Courier-Journal, 21 April 1889.

commercial and cultural superior. *Harper's New Monthly Magazine* (Vol. 77) in 1888 commented that:

> In its physical aspect Louisville is in every respect a contrast to Cincinnati. Lying on a plain, sloping gently up from the river, it spreads widely in rectangular uniformity of streets—a city of broad avenues, getting to be well paved and well shaded, with ample spaces in lawns, houses detached, somewhat uniform in style, but with an air of comfort, occasionally of elegance and solid good taste. The city has an exceedingly open, friendly, cheerful appearance. In May, with its abundant foliage and flowery lawns, it is a beautiful city: a beautiful, healthful city in a temperate climate, surrounded by a fertile country, is Louisville . . . But the contrast of Cincinnati and Louisville in social life and in the manner of doing business cannot all be accounted for by Blue-Grass. It would be very interesting, if one had the knowledge, to study the causes of this contrast in two cities not very far apart. In late years Louisville has awakened to a new commercial life, as one finds in it a strong infusion of Western business energy and ambition. It is jubilant in its growth and prosperity.

Servant on steps of the Herman Verhoeff Jr. House, *ca.* 1893.

Louisville was changing drastically. Two years later *Harper's Weekly* (5 April 1890) also detailed the city's commercial interests, emphasizing its manufacturing enterprises.

> In the matter of shipping and manufacturing, the tobacco industry here ranks first. It is claimed that one-third of all the tobacco grown in North America is handled by the warehouses of Louisville. There are in the city eighteen tobacco warehouses, thirteen rehandling establishments, sixteen manufactories of chewing and smoking tobacco, and seventy-nine cigar factories.
>
> Statistics show that Louisville has 1100 manufacturing establishments, which employ 39,000 people, and turn out products valued at $65,000,000.

The Verhoeff House on the southeast corner of Second and Jacob streets, shown *ca.* 1893, was demolished in 1975. The Frank N. Hartwell House (*ca.* 1883) at right with Eastlake decoration is the site of Master Hosts Inn.

Train running west on Maple at Eleventh St. about 1893. Verhoeff's grain elevator at left was reportedly the first (1875) in Louisville.

West side of Eleventh at Cottage
Alley (between Maple and Broadway)
about 1893.

Walnut Street Baptist Church had moved to the southeast corner of Third and St. Catherine streets when shown in 1906. Châteauesque style house at right (1123 Third St.) was designed by Maury & Dodd.

The products in the manufacture of which Louisville claims superiority to the rest of the country are, in addition to tobacco, jeans, jeans clothing, cast gas and water pipes, ploughs, cement, oak-tanned leather, plate-glass, and fine whiskeys. In the production of this late-named article Louisville has a wide-spread reputation. What is asserted to be the largest wagon manufactory in the world is located here. The transportation facilities for the shipment of manufactured goods are exceptionally good by both rail and water. Some of the largest railway systems of the country have connections here, while in the matter of water transportation it is said that thirty navigable rivers are accessible from the Louisville wharves.

The substantial proprietary and managerial class forged by this commercial boom, as well as a growing number of professional people, wanted to reside conveniently near their industrial plants and office buildings. The large, flat farm plain just south of the center city invited residential development. By extending cross streets and creating new east-west avenues, the area was made accessible. Blocks were evenly subdivided into building lots which produced a uniform, homogeneous and, by contemporary standards, a rather unpretentious neighborhood. As *Harper's Weekly* also reiterated in 1890:

> The residence sections extend back over a broad plateau, which is elevated about seventy feet above the level of the river at ordinary stages of water. The streets cross one another at right angles, and so great has been the care bestowed upon them that in the summer they have the appearance of shaded drives in a park. Many of the houses that look out from the breaks in the long rows of well-grown shade trees are in the highest degree creditable to modern architecture, but the prevailing style of residence gives one the restful impression that the homes of Louisville were built with the idea of comfort and convenience. As a rule each house has a plot of ground

Parlor of the Green House, 1032
Fourth St., *ca.* 1905.

of its own, and this plot is in almost every instance embellished with trees and shrubbery, and beautified with flowers. The effect upon the visitor who sees none of these things at home, but whose life is mostly spent in the barren streets of New York or Chicago, is indescribably restful and charming. One would, indeed, be justified in saying that the chief glory of Louisville is to be found in the beautiful residence thoroughfares.

Louisville Police Captain Michael Barry in front of his grape arbor at 633 St. Catherine, *ca.* 1903.

Opposite: Carriage in front of the Samuel A. Culbertson House, 1432 Third St. Photographed by Klauber shortly after it was built about 1897.

Residential construction continued to flourish in Old Louisville during the Gay Nineties, despite some slackening caused by shock waves from the 1890 tornado. Those individuals who possessed the standards and means to reflect their social and financial positions, did so.

Why then within several decades did the leading families feel compelled to move from such a stately neighborhood? Why were their magnificent homes partitioned into multi-family units? Why did Old Louisville ultimately deteriorate into an Urban Renewal district? The answer is contained in its very name—*Old* Louisville. The derivation of the term apparently has been forgotten, but it seems to have become widely accepted between World War I and the Depression. The term is obviously anachronistic, since other sections of the city had existed for generations prior to residential encroachment on the farm lots south of Broadway. But more importantly, Old Louisville had a negative overtone as well as a chronological connotation. In an era when architectural styles were changing dramatically, *Old* meant out of fashion.

Lifestyles were being modified overnight too. The advent of automobiles eliminated horses, carriages, and wagons. Detached carriage houses were replaced by garages attached to houses for convenience. Significant developments in gas, electricity, plumbing, sewers, heat, and light were being made constantly. Resulting internal conveniences began to eliminate the need for servants who were finding better-paying industrial jobs anyway. There was great social motivation to live in houses with stylish appearances.

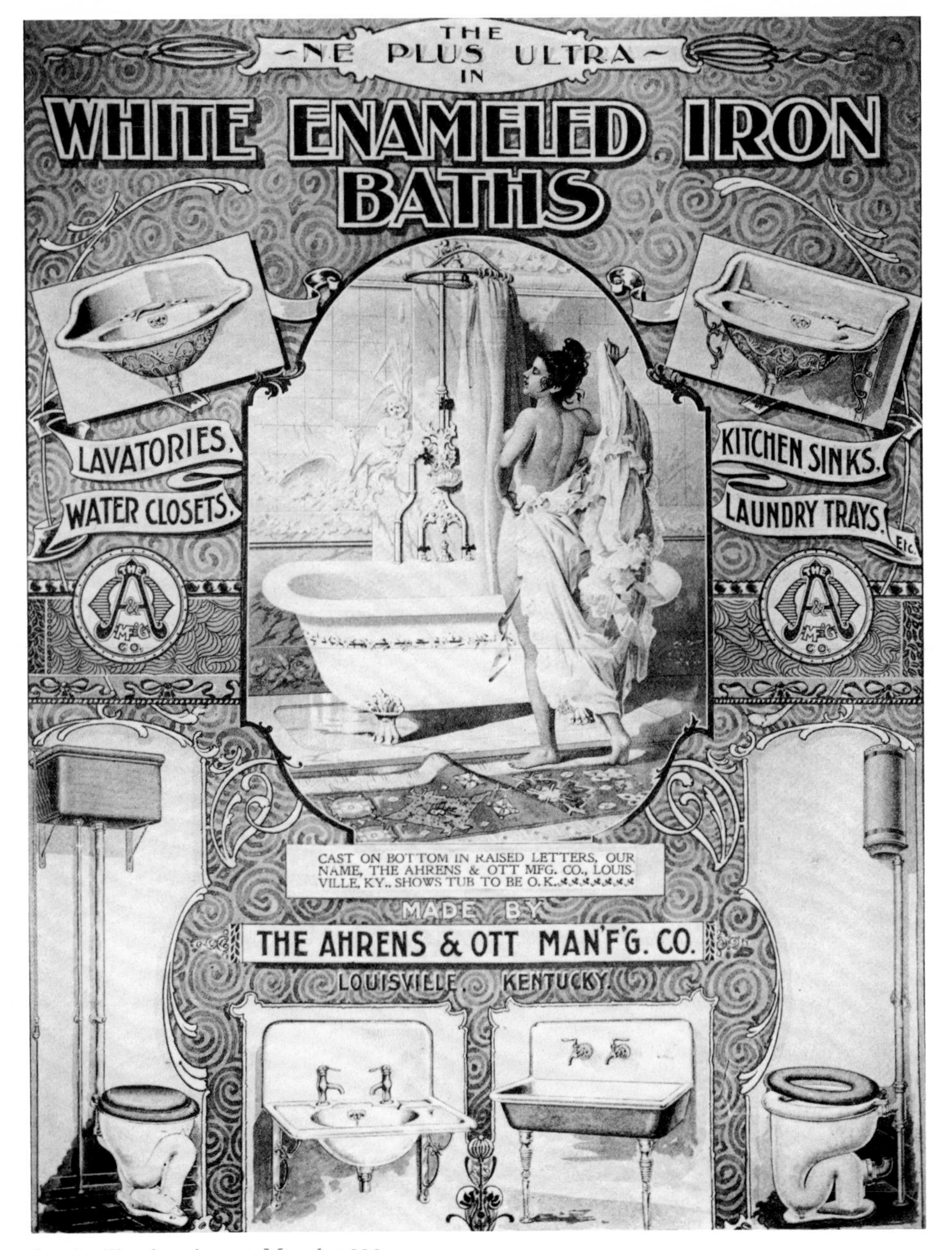

Louisville Anzeiger, 1 March 1898.

Opposite: Pinckney F. Green in his library at 1032 Fourth St., *ca.* 1907.

But by 1910, houses in the newest styles incorporating the most modern conveniences were not being built in Old Louisville mainly because the most attractive lots already had been taken. The well-to-do could afford to purchase the most advantageous building sites in the undeveloped periphery preferably overlooking one of the new city parks or along one of the connecting boulevards. With better means of transportation at their disposal, they did not have to live near downtown, and could reside just as conveniently in the Highlands or some other outlying scenic section.

Eventually the first families abandoned Old Louisville, and absentee landlords carved up their residential holdings into multi-family units.

After the Second World War, even St. James and Belgravia courts—the last vestiges of owner occupied residences —appeared doomed to becoming a rooming house district. But encouraged by the farsighted St. James Court Association, interest in reviving the neighborhood began to mount. In the early 1960s, the Old Louisville Association, Inc. was formed to promote the rehabilitation of the historic and scenic urban district. An offshoot organization, Restoration, Inc., moved directly into the fray by purchasing dilapidated structures along Belgravia Court for renovation. This example induced others to recongregate in the picturesque neighborhood.

The task of stabilizing and revitalizing Old Louisville has been long and arduous and not without setbacks and losses of significant structures. But with the support of the Neighborhood Development Corporation and other on-the-scene self-help groups, reuse of existing housing near downtown is being achieved. Old Louisville's preservation thus goes beyond simply saving a picturesque legacy of the Victorian era. It enhances the quality of life of the community at large and it contributes to the continuing renewal of the adjacent downtown.

The Quest for a
Lost Race

A Legacy in Architecture

by William Morgan

The boundaries of Old Louisville frame an architectural mosaic of tremendous stylistic variety and incredible visual richness which constitutes one of the most outstanding collections of Victorian domestic architecture in America. Victorian architecture, which appeals to the emotions rather than the intellect, is characterized by lavishness, complexity, color, and picturesqueness, and these features as well as the stylistic elements and phases of what is called "Victorian" can be found in Old Louisville. The bold buildings of the post-Civil War period mirrored national self-confidence. They reflect more meaningfully the country's maturity than do the transplanted and venerated English Georgian designs of two centuries ago, and as such are equally worthy of pride. A strong case can even be made for Victorian as a national style. But many Americans regard "Victorian" as a synonym for ugliness, partly because the architecture of one generation is rarely appreciated by succeeding generations. To many, Victorian houses are the dark, foreboding, and often over-furnished dwellings of their grandparents. Without the patina of age to protect them, many of these houses are not considered as special objects to be preserved, but merely as out-moded buildings of a less-enlightened time.

Fortunately, a growing number of Americans are beginning to understand the historical and intrinsic merits of late-nineteenth-century architecture. All architectural styles of the past are important to the identity not only of a city but in large measure to the country as well. The issue is not one of transient taste—of beauty as one generation defines it—but of preserving the complete fabric of history. Yet along with this understanding comes the realization that much of America's Victorian heritage has been destroyed in the name of progress. Far more structures were built in the late nineteenth century than in the eighteenth, but this fact only made Victorian buildings more vulnerable. While the homes of founding fathers were preserved—or even reconstructed—the houses of our grandfathers suffered what has amounted to patrimonial genocide. In this respect, Louisville is more fortunate than other cities, though it should be noted that those buildings which have survived to the present day represent a fragment of what was Old Louisville at

Third St. north from Burnett, 1897.

Above left: 1424 Fourth St., 1961.
Center: 130 W. Ormsby, 1961.
Right: 1332 Fourth St., 1961.
Below left: 1375 Fourth St., 1961.
Center: 1314 Third St., 1961.
Right: 1375 Fourth St., 1961.

Opposite: 1423 Fourth St., 1961.

the beginning of this century. Many of the houses illustrated here, such as the very handsome ones that lined Broadway (*p. 148*) and adjoining streets, have long since been obliterated by commercial development. However, the remaining Victorian structures in Old Louisville are numerous and diverse enough to provide one of the best documents for the study and appreciation of this long-neglected part of the country's architectural heritage.

The houses of Old Louisville illustrate the variety and range of Victorian styles and, in fact, their stylistic and chronological development follows a southward migration and can be very broadly traced by location and time: Italianate (1850s and 1860s) and Victorian Gothic (late 1870s and 1880s) along Broadway; Richardsonian Romanesque and Queen Anne (1880s and 1890s) roughly from Kentucky to Central Park; Châteauesque and Renaissance Revival (1895-1905) from Ormsby to Hill streets, and so forth. Within the general stylistic categories can be found decorative details from any number of historical sources—Baroque, Rococo, Flemish, Eastlake, President Grant, Second Empire, Moorish, Venetian, and Jacobean. Often these different styles are blended together in one structure. Such eclecticism, with its frank and unabashed use of past forms, makes the Victorian style—especially that found in Old Louisville—what is most vital about American architecture. Even so, there have been historians who have contended that this practice of borrowing and mixing is dishonest. Still, without being bound by overly academic definitions, those various stylistic factors that contribute to the picturesqueness of Old Louisville can be surveyed.

Perhaps the strongest thread that runs through all nineteenth-century architecture is the romantic one. Whereas eighteenth-century builders stressed symmetry and proportion —that is, the inherent qualities of the object itself—nineteenth-century architects emphasized the emotional responses which the structure aroused in the spectator. Architectural symbolism is familiar to the viewer whether one is conscious of it or not. For example, Greek columns identify such civic structures as banks and courthouses, while Gothic spires identify churches.

Row Houses, *ca.* 1870, on the southeast corner of Second and St. Catherine streets, 1961.

Opposite top: J. F. Buckner built this house on the southeast corner of Brook and College streets *ca.* 1864. It later served the Roman Catholic Diocese of Louisville as the home for their bishop, Our Lady's Home for Infants, and the Catholic Charities Agency. Demolished. Bottom: Built *ca.* 1858 by W. B. Hamilton at 620 Third St., south of Chestnut, this house later was owned by the Rt. Rev. T. U. Dudley, Bishop of the Protestant Episcopal Diocese of Kentucky. Demolished.

Yet private dwellings are perhaps more reflective of change in taste and fashion than religious or civic monuments, and in the nineteenth century for the first time domestic structures assumed an architectural and cultural importance equal to that of public buildings.

As romantic and as associative as a Greek temple might be (with its references to the birthplace of democracy and identification with the Greek War of Independence), its popularity as a house style was waning in the 1850s. This was in large part because the temple plan, like the Georgian layout that preceded it, was based on ideas of classical symmetry. It did not differentiate rooms by their function, nor was it flexible enough to accommodate new developments in kitchen design or the introduction of indoor plumbing.

The reaction against the Greek Revival style for domestic architecture was led by Andrew Jackson Downing, the horticulturist and polemicist, whose books—*Treatise on the Theory and Practice of Landscape Gardening*, *Cottage Residences*, and *the Architecture of Country Houses* (published in 1841, 1842, and 1850 respectively)—were the most popular of their kind published by an American. Downing revolutionized the American house by offering design sketches with irregular and asymmetrical layouts instead of axial plans. (His explanation of and plea for picturesque planning principles also affected landscape design, as can be seen in Louisville's great park system created by Frederick Law Olmsted, a Downing follower.)

One of the open-plan styles advocated by Downing (and other writers of contemporary builders guides) as both picturesque and practical was the Italian Villa. The flexibility of this style made it extremely popular and it is one of the mainstays of house types in Old Louisville. The plan usually consisted of two or more asymmetrical blocks flanking a tower [Moorman House (*p. 21*)], which was theoretically for the view and consequently was often under-emphasized or omitted altogether in urban residences like the Robinson-DuPont House (*p. 34*). Stuccoed walls, like those of the Tuscan farmhouse upon which the style was based, were preferred, but any material could be used to offset a variety of window moldings,

cornice brackets, or porches—all details that tended to become more elaborate with time. In fact, there are almost as many variants of the style as there are villas in Old Louisville; the free and comfortable plan obviously provided an ideal suburban style.

The Buckner House built on Brook Street (*p. 57*) has smooth walls, round-headed windows, and a peaked gable in the center of the main facade which identify it as an Italian Villa derived from Downing. The elaborate cast-iron porch was added later. Similarly, the columns supporting the porch on the residence of W. B. Hamilton (*p. 57*) appear to have been cast iron, but the octagonal tower-like bay has been placed to the side. Unlike their European counterparts, American cottages and villas featured porches or verandas, a characteristic native contribution ideally suited to outside social activities centered around rocking chairs and swings. The size and importance of the porch grew with time and the one on the Smith-Lithgow House (*p. 94*) has been extended across the facade and wrapped around the sides. The Avery House (*p. 94*) is yet another example of this Tuscan style.

Another Italian mode appeared in Louisville shortly before the Civil War, but the model was the astylar (or columnless) urban palace of High Renaissance Rome and Florence, rather than the rural farmhouse of Tuscany. The houses by the Irish-trained Henry Whitestone, such as the Ford-Green Mansion of *ca.* 1858 (*59, 92, 93*) the Newcomb Mansion of the following year (*p. 93*), and Standiford House, *ca.* 1880 (*p. 94*) are excellent examples and show the sophisticated vocabulary Whitestone learned from association with the famous New York architect Isaiah Rogers. Far more palatial and costly, and thus less numerous, these High Renaissance-inspired houses—like the Robinson-Wheeler-Landward House (*p. 60, 150*) and the residence of B. F. Guthrie (*p. 133*)—tend to be symmetrical, frontal rectangular blocks, usually topped by a strong cornice, while the porches are no longer spacious verandas but are treated as monumental entrances. Detailing is more classical and the facades are rarely left smooth, the local limestone lending itself to heavy quoining and rustication. The fact that lime-

The *ca.* 1875 residence of plow manufacturer Benjamin F. Avery on the southeast corner of Fourth and Broadway, housed the Y.M.C.A. from 1897 until 1913. Shown in 1897, it is the site of the Heyburn Building.

Opposite: The James C. Ford Mansion, designed by Henry Whitestone, was built *ca.* 1858 on the southwest corner of Second and Broadway. It was owned later by Dr. Norvin Green and used by the Y.W.C.A. Photographed in 1955, it was demolished in 1964 for the Portland Federal Building. The heavy rustication on the first floor contrasted with the smooth surface of the second floor is characteristic of the Renaissance Revival style.

WORLD
ELKS

The Renaissance Revival style Robinson-Wheeler-Landward House, erected *ca.* 1872 on the northeast corner of Fourth and Magnolia, is shown prior to 1910.

Opposite top: The Edward Watts Chamberlain House (*ca.* 1888) was located on the southwest corner of Fourth and Oak streets. Shown *ca.* 1890, it is now the site of a First National Bank branch. Note the slender columns set within the deeply recessed window frames. Bottom: Built *ca.* 1876 by Sid N. Platt and later owned by Abner E. Norman, this house at 1357 Fourth St. is now the site of the Park Central Apartments. The intricately incised window decoration was machine carved.

stone facing is often limited to the street front (as on the Norman House at 1357 Fourth Street, *p. 61*) is in keeping with the urban source of the style.

A combination of the two Italian styles, with their well-defined cornices, multifarious brackets, brick or limestone fronts, round-headed windows, and, invariably, a three-bay facade with doorway to one side, can be found throughout Old Louisville. Two examples, now destroyed, are the Chamberlain House (*p. 61*) and the Winter residence at 1000 Third Street (*p. 62*). These types are the Louisville equivalent to the Brownstones so characteristic of New York City at that period, although the dressed and light-colored limestone, as on the Verhoeff House (*p. 68*), gives the local version a greater air of elegance and urbanity than the more somber New Jersey sandstone which tends to flake and chip. The difference between the Tuscan and Roman Italian style in these buildings depends on whether there is a projecting bay (a reference to the tower) or a flat surface. However their exact stylistic lineage becomes academic in the post-Civil War period when historical accuracy begins to break down and the marvelous nineteenth-century hybrids with even less illuminating labels like Franco-Italian, Swiss Cottage, and Anglo-Norman are produced.

Similar confusion prevails when the other popular Victorian styles are viewed. Is, for example, the Samuel Miller House (*p. 64*) French or Italian? The unique Victorian character of such a building is not always easily ascertained by defining its constituent stylistic elements, for the asymmetrical plan and central tower of the Miller residence are clearly Italian, yet its mansard roof is one of the hallmarks of the Second Empire Style associated with the reign of Napoleon III in France. Second Empire was so popular in the 1870s for public buildings [like the Philadelphia City Hall, the Executive Office Building in Washington, Louisville's City Hall, Bull Block (*p. 98*), Industrial Exposition, (*p.28*), Female High School (*p. 105*) and Masonic Home (*p. 107*)] that it was regarded almost as the official American style. The French style was just as fashionable for residential structures. Frequently the same builders' guide

Very similar in treatment to the Chamberlain House (*p. 61*) is Julius Winter's home built *ca.* 1885 on the southwest corner of Third and Kentucky streets. It was later the Standard Club before being demolished.

Left: The Herman Verhoeff, Jr. House (*ca.* 1879) on the southeast corner of Second and Jacob streets, shown *ca.* 1893. The architectural components are clearly articulated in keeping with Renaissance classicism. The house is contained between a solid base and a strong cornice. Each floor is delineated by a belt course and the upper stories are defined vertically by corner pilasters. The doorway is framed by a heavy entablature and proportionately short engaged columns—a treatment that became more pronounced in later Victorian styles and culminated in the stocky columns of the Richardsonian Romanesque. Above: Home of William H. Fosdick (*ca.* 1878) at 1132 Third St., between St. Catherine and Oak streets, *ca.* 1893.

which delineated the Italianate offered a duplicate design with the addition of the square-domed, or mansard, roof.

It is oftentimes pedantic and unfruitful to identify component sources of a Victorian house. For example, the mansard roof on the Miller House is decorated with High Victorian Gothic details: a crested railing and polychromed striped tiles. Victorian architects further obscured the stylistic lineage of their designs by the free use of transitional styles; that is, a style in the process of evolving into another one. In short, the Victorian builder delighted in the elements of variety and serendipity, along with the romantic and the picturesque and, of course, the exotic.

Just when Americans were celebrating a century of political independence, their architectural imagination was fired by the British fashion for High Victorian Gothic. John Ruskin, the English art critic and arbiter of taste who was so widely read in America, extended the revival of Gothic forms through his championing of Venetian architecture. The decaying Queen of the Adriatic, being a blend of East and West, Gothic, Renaissance, and Byzantine, offered an ideal source for the Victorian architect in search of novelty. The Dillingham House (*p. 67*), which stood on Broadway, with its sharply pointed, deeply recessed lancet windows, quatrefoils, and picturesque skyline composed of towers, spires, dormers, and roof crestings, and its neighbor, the Long residence (*p. 66*), were superb examples of High Victorian Gothic. In addition to Venetian forms—pointed arches, classical columns, Baroque scrolls—the real attraction was color: polychromy achieved by employing different colored materials. (Note the contrasting of smooth stone trim with rough masonry walls on the Dillingham House.) Although the details are more Italianate than Venetian, the Peaslee-Farnsley House (*p. 95*) employed towers, dormers, and contrasting masonry to similar effect.

Almost as exuberant, and certainly as free in the use of irregular plans, picturesque massing, and color, was the Queen Anne style. The name however, is anachronistic, for the style was not in any way associated with that early eighteenth-century monarch, but was based on the Elizabethan. The

Opposite: Samuel A. Miller's home (*ca.* 1883) at 1236 Fourth St. is the site of the Puritan Apartments. Shown in 1889, it is an excellent example of the French Second Empire style, with its fishscale shingled mansard (or square-dome) roof and decorative iron cresting. Despite the pronounced bracketed cornice beneath the roof and the similar treatment of the belt course above the first story, the overall verticality is emphasized by the tall proportions and the narrow windows. Also typical of the style are the almost flat window arches and the circular bull's-eye keystones on the attic windows.

Left: Crowd gathered at the St. Louis Bertrand School (*ca.* 1866), 1122 Sixth St., during a St. Patrick's Day celebration, *ca.* 1915. The unusual double-pitched dormers on the bell-shaped mansard roof have been removed. The window moldings and cornice are simply painted brick instead of carved stone. P. J. Keeley and N. J. Murphy were the architects.

John S. Long's residence (*ca.* 1865) at 212 W. Broadway between Second and Third streets, was enlarged and improved *ca.* 1882. It is shown about 1920 when used by the DeMolay Commandery No. 12, and is the site of the Portland Federal Building. The Long House is practically identical to the Verhoeff House (*p. 63*) except for the use of Gothic arches which reflects the Dillingham House next door.

Built *ca.* 1877 at 214 W. Broadway by mill and factory supplier W. H. Dillingham, this house shown about 1885 is presently the site of the Dizzy Whizz Downtowner. In general layout, the Dillingham House is very similar to the Samuel Miller residence (*p. 64*), however, the decorative program is obviously Gothic rather than Renaissance in inspiration.

Trellis decoration on a terra-cotta panel, 1328 Fourth St., 1961.

models were usually rural manor houses of the turn of the seventeenth century and were basically late medieval with Renaissance details. For the Victorian they had an added attraction, that of employing different materials on one surface, such as half-timber, a combination of wood and brick.

Largely the creation of the English architect Richard Norman Shaw, the Queen Anne style was imported to this country by the British delegation to the Philadelphia Centennial where the two half-timbered cottages they erected were among the most admired buildings of the 1876 Exposition. Thus Americans, who did not find their own past distant enough to be sufficiently romantic, were given a style in which they could indulge in all manner of turrets, towers, over-hanging gables, oriel or bay windows, and huge multi-stack chimneys. The G. H. Hoertz House (*p. 96*) was regarded by contemporaries as one of the most outstanding Queen Anne style residences in Louisville. Beneath picturesque medieval rooflines, Queen Anne houses were constructed with as many surface modulations as possible. While half-timbering and tile were not used as extensively in Old Louisville as elsewhere, wood shingles were ideal for similar effects, which are well-illustrated by the Louisville Athletic Club (*p. 32*) and the Ballard House (*p. 70*). Queen Anne houses tended to use materials with harmonious color combinations of reds and browns—brick, sandstone, terra-cotta, sandstone carved to look like terra-cotta—which counterbalanced the surface variations and thus avoided the discordancy of some of the other late-Victorian styles.

The Queen Anne style mated classical details with medieval ones, often to excellent effect. A tower or wall dormer may be terminated by a segmental or triangular pediment or some other Georgian form (as on the Ballard House), or a classical entablature may be adorned with Victorian decoration (as on the *ca.* 1888 Semple House, *p. 71*).

Some of the finest Queen Anne ornament is to be found on the Russell Houston House (*p. 15, 73, 137*) at the corner of Fourth Street and Park Avenue by Louisville architect Mason Maury, designer of such advanced structures as the Kaufman-Straus Building and the demolished Kenyon Build-

The Graham Macfarlane residence (*ca.* 1888) on the southwest corner of Second and Ormsby illustrates the variety of fenestration and roof treatments possible in a Queen Anne house. Note the drain basins beneath the chimney. Mrs. L. L. Dorsey's home (*ca.* 1887) next door has another Queen Anne feature—a half-timbered peaked gable.

Samuel Thruston Ballard, lieutenant governor of Kentucky from 1919-1923, built his home at 415 E. Broadway *ca.* 1887. The Ballard House, now demolished, demonstrated dramatically the flair with which Queen Anne architects used shingle. The shingle covering the second story is treated like a thin membrane stretched across the varied surfaces.

Built by railway supplier William Semple (*ca.* 1888), this house is at 1209 Third St. between Oak and Ormsby. The semi-elliptical pediment of the wall dormer and the porch are Classical forms, but they are decorated with the free-flowing floral motifs that are one of the identifying hallmarks of the Queen Anne style.

Interlacing pediment ornamentation typical of Queen Anne decoration, 1328 Fourth St., 1961.

ing (*p. 98*), and perhaps the most prolific builder of residential architecture in the city. But this house and its neighbor to the north are at the same time among the finest Richardsonian Romanesque Revival houses extant in this country. And if Old Louisville—and the city as a whole—gave its heart to one style more than any other, it was to the revival of Romanesque forms inspired by one of America's greatest and most imitated architects, Henry Hobson Richardson.

Romanesque forms had been used before in America, and Richardson himself began with High Victorian and even did some Queen Anne, but he employed the round arches and massive masonry of that French medieval style as the basic motif for the creation of a totally new expression. Richardson's brilliant career was cut short by his untimely death at 48 in 1886, but his tremendously powerful buildings were copied by architects and builders in every American city for the next decade.

Old Louisville has some truly outstanding examples of Richardsonian Romanesque, such as the K. W. Smith House (*p. 73*), the Robinson House (*p. 74*), and the Theophilus Conrad House (*p. 75*) on St. James Court. "Conrad's Folly" (built in 1893-4 by Arthur Loomis, a local architect who trained with Henry Whitestone), with its incredible profusion of carved detail—gargoyles, swags, arabesques, foliated capitals—on the exterior and the equally rich interiors of light oak, marble, and stained glass, is one of the great undiscovered American houses and should be regarded as one of Louisville's principle architectural landmarks.

Richardsonian became the pre-eminent domestic style in the southern part of Old Louisville, and though rarely on the scale of the Conrad House, handsome examples such as the Selliger residence (*p. 76*) attest to its popularity. In fact, the style was such a favorite here that it lasted into the early years of this century, long beyond its vogue in other cities. The round arch (especially for entrance doorways and porches) is perhaps the most characteristic detail of the entire Old Louisville neighborhood, and it is even found on houses as the only embellishment on an otherwise plain facade. Local limestone was ideally suited for arches and the "stonier than stone" fortification-like

Above: Northwest corner of Fourth and Park Avenue. On the Russell Houston House (*ca.* 1887) on the corner, architect Mason Maury used red stone trim—quoining, belt courses, lintels, sills, and columns—to unify a picturesque massing of brick into a powerful composition of tremendous originality. The adjacent house still under construction for Williamson Bacon and Claude Barnes in 1888, is a notable example of Richardsonian Romanesque style with its masonry porch and projecting round bays. Left: Also designed by Mason Maury is the K. W. Smith House (*ca.* 1888) at 1118 Third St. that now houses the Dougherty Funeral Home. The masonry facade gives this Queen Anne house a Romanesque appearance. Unlike the monochromatic Houston House, Maury used a variety of harmonious colored materials in the Smith House.

The home George A. Robinson built *ca.* 1885 at 1015 Fourth St. is an early example of the Romanesque Revival in Louisville. The massive round arches supported by short, stubby columns and the round projecting bay topped with a conical roof are typical of the Richardsonian style. It was designed by C. J. Clarke and Arthur Loomis.

Left: Theophilus Conrad built his home on the corner of St. James Ct. and Magnolia *ca.* 1894. Called by contemporaries "Conrad's Folly," it is the Rose Anna Hughes Presbyterian Home. A notable example of domestic Richardsonian Romanesque, the Conrad House employs ashlar masonry throughout. The paired arches of the porch, with their carved voussoirs and foliated capitals, and the grouping of three columns on the third story are motifs borrowed from works by the style's progenitor, Henry Hobson Richardson. Top: Detail from the Conrad House, 1402 St. James Ct., 1961. Bottom: 1416 Third St., 1961.

masonry espoused by Richardson (like the Stine-Bernheim House of 1886 designed by Mason Maury, *p. 77*), but the style was so pervasive that it was used just as extensively in brick and even in wood. Old Louisville contains what surely must be one of the more noteworthy and well-preserved collections of Richardsonian Romanesque in the United States.

As popular as the style was—Richardsonian Romanesque was one of the few American fashions imitated by Europeans—its chief feature, the simple masonry arch, allowed only limited variation. An example of experimentation with the arch form can be seen on the J. T. Gathright House (*p. 77*) where a large brick arch has been bent elliptically, with the result that the rather forced shape is more Georgian than Romanesque.

Yet another French-inspired mode was the Châteauesque, based on the late Gothic-early Renaissance style prevalent in the early sixteenth century. It was introduced largely through the efforts of Richard Morris Hunt who, like Richardson, had studied at the prestigious, classically oriented École des Beaux Arts in Paris. Hunt developed a reputation as a society architect by designing such notable chateaux as the William K. Vanderbilt Mansion in New York, Ochre Court in Newport, and Biltmore near Asheville, North Carolina. While none of the Old Louisville examples of Châteauesque are as grand or as pretentious as those by Hunt, they do share the same lively outlines and characteristic academic details: round or square turrets, steep-pitched gables and wall dormers, basket-handle arches for windows, doorways and porches such as the examples by Maury & Dodd (*p. 49, 79*), and window openings mullioned in the shape of a Latin cross, as found on the residence of P. H. Tapp (*p. 78*). Although the more famous designs like Biltmore are modeled after great country palaces like Blois and Chambord, inspiration also came from the urban houses of the new merchant class, and thus are particularly appropriate to Old Louisville.

In some of the Old Louisville examples of the Châteauesque, such as the group of houses at Fourth and Hill streets (*p. 80*), the curving French forms are abandoned in favor of more linear treatment, the roof dormers owing more to late-

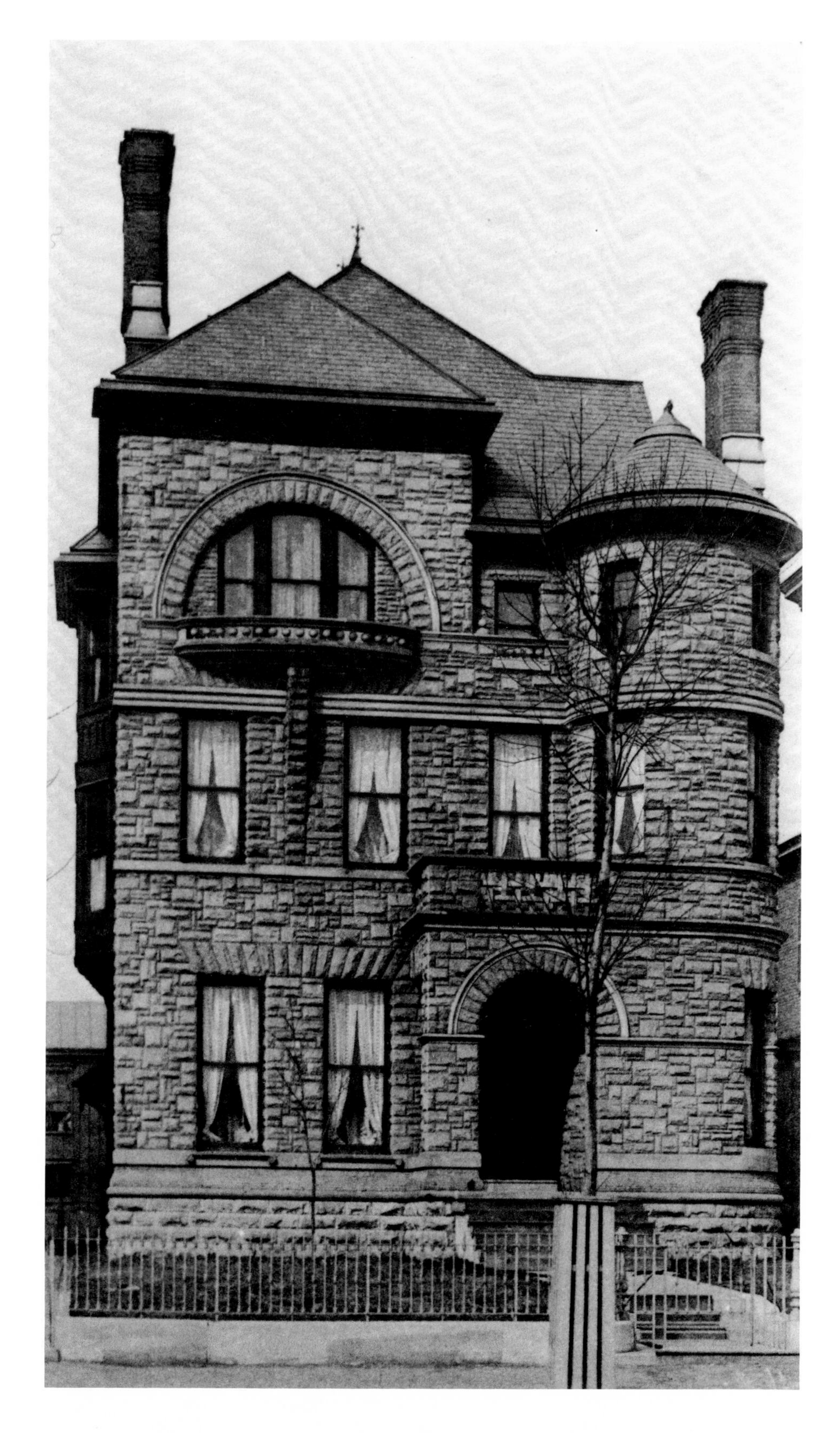

Left: The Stine-Bernheim House (*ca.* 1886), designed by Mason Maury, was built originally for O. T. Sutfield and still stands at 1014 Third St. Above: Now demolished, the J. T. Gathright residence was erected at 1111 Third St., between St. Catherine and Oak, *ca.* 1889. Built less expensively with brick, the Gathright House is a more modest example of the Richardsonian Romanesque, although it has stone trim. The wooden porch, which appears delicate in comparison to the massiveness of the rest of the structure, is similar to others used in Old Louisville.

Opposite: The Max Selliger House, 1022 Third St. (*ca.* 1888), illustrates the variety of surface pattern achievable with limestone.

Above: Built by Presley H. Tapp *ca.* 1888 at 429 W. Ormsby, this house is the site of the Mayflower Apartments. While the Tapp House retains an asymmetrical layout and a medieval verticality, the classical details suggest a renewing interest in Renaissance styles.

Opposite: Fourth St. looking north toward Park, 1897. Somewhat more medieval than the Tapp House, Miss Mary Lafon's *ca.* 1891 residence at the right (now a parking lot) demonstrates the characteristic features of the Châteauesque—basket-handle arches, cross-shaped windows and pointed wall dormers.

Above: 200 W. Ormsby, 1961. The salamander was the symbol of Francis I, whose reign fostered the architecture termed Châteauesque.

Gothic architecture of the Low Countries. While the medieval architecture of Belgium did not inspire many nineteenth-century buildings, Norton Hall of the old Southern Baptist Theological Seminary (*p. 81*), with its abundance of little conical dormers and majestic central tower, must have been one of the finest recreations of a late-medieval Flemish town hall.

Some architects following Hunt and Richardson received their training in Paris, while those unable to go abroad studied at the new American architecture schools which were founded in the 1870s and 1880s and modeled on the classical principles of the École. Certain houses built in the 1890s in Old Louisville began to show evidence of this classical training. The Ainslee House 1215 Third St. and the Samuel Grabfelder House (the work of architects Dodd & Cobb, *p. 143*) demonstrate a more refined and restrained approach; the profusion of Victorian ornament is replaced by sparing use of Italian Renaissance Revival detail.

These houses are illustrative of the Academic Reaction (sometimes referred to as the "American Renaissance") that began as early as the 1880s but really flowered in the first quarter of this century. The "Reaction" was a response to what was believed by some to be the over-excesses of the Victorian styles, their over-reliance on colorful complexity, and their lack of "purity." The Edwin Hite Ferguson House (*p. 83*), also designed by William Dodd, at one time an associate of Mason Maury and designer of the old Louisville Presbyterian Theological Seminary (now Jefferson Community College) and Arthur Cobb in 1901, with its strict symmetry and classicistic-Baroque detailing is not dissimilar to Parisian houses of the period—its grandeur more suited to the pretentions of America's Gilded Age robber barons than to Louisville's management class. Non-domestic examples of this academic Neo-Classicism include the Louisville Free Public Library of 1907 (by George Tachau and Lewis Pilcher) and the J. B. Speed Art Museum (one of the last works by Arthur Loomis who had abandoned the Richardsonian Romanesque of "Conrad's Folly," the Levy Brothers Building, and the University of Louisville Medical College), and also Memorial Auditorium (designed by nationally prominent

Above: Fourth looking north from Hill St., 1903. These five *ca.* 1897 houses form a notable Châteauesque ensemble and illustrate the transitional nature of the style's source. Each is decorated with numerous late-Gothic and early-Renaissance details. Although the treatment of the dormers on each house is different, they all contribute to a remarkably unified and very picturesque effect. The Mary Lyman House (*ca.* 1897) to the north was destroyed by fire in 1973. Right: 1365 Third St., 1961.

Opposite: Norton Hall was constructed on the south side of Broadway between Fourth and Fifth streets *ca.* 1895. Demolished.

1314 Third St., 1961.

Opposite: Built by oil refiner Edwin H. Ferguson *ca.* 1905 at 1310 Third St., this Beaux-Arts house is now the L. D. Pearson & Son Funeral Home. Architects Dodd and Cobb employed a range of elaborate classical and Baroque details within a symmetrical and controlled facade to produce a formal and elegant composition. The house's symmetry and restraint illustrate the growing influence of Parisian academic training and the rejection of the Victorian preference for asymmetry and medieval sources. Shown in 1955, the house next door (now demolished) was also built by Ferguson about 1896.

Thomas Hastings). The Speed Museum and Memorial Auditorium are both products of the 1920s.

Eventually, even the Colonial and Georgian styles were revived. Colonial and neo-Georgian details—Palladian windows, columned porches, scalloped and segmental pediments—began to appear throughout Old Louisville. (*p. 85, p. 139, p. 140*). Usually these were treated in a free Victorian manner and were often added to existing nineteenth-century houses. The Madison Cawein House at 1436 St. James Court, with its gracefully-bowed front and elliptical fanlight, is an example of the late-Georgian or Federal style, although it is a Victorian house that was remodeled. Larger, non-domestic Georgian examples, such as the Law School, the Speed Scientific School, and the Jeffersonian Pantheon of the Administration Building, are features of the 1927-1929 plan of the Belknap Campus of the University of Louisville laid out principally by Louisville architects Frederic L. Morgan and Arthur Tafel, Sr. and expanded in 1933 by the nationally famous campus planner, Jens Frederick Larson. The Belknap Campus chronologically as well as geographically marks the outer limits of what is now considered Old Louisville, and the Colonial Revival is associated more with neighborhoods developed after Old Louisville, such as the Cherokee Triangle area.

Because development had ceased for the most part around the turn of the century, more modern and progressive, non-historical styles are found less in Old Louisville than in newer suburbs. Old Louisville does have a few smaller bungalows, midwestern versions of the California Mission style. Generally the more modern fashions are limited to details, such as stained glass, rustic iron door hinges, and the use of Arts and Crafts style interiors found in the St. James-Belgravia area—the blond oak "Craftsman" furniture in contrast to the heavier Victorian stained-grained mahogany.

Except for embellishments, the seeds of modernism should not be sought in Old Louisville, although we perhaps should be reminded that the great pioneers of modern architecture were Victorians. Frank Lloyd Wright's early works were Colonial Revival houses in the Chicago suburbs, and his

master, Louis Sullivan, decorated his steel-framed skyscrapers with incredibly rich ornament not dissimilar to that found in Old Louisville. Nor should the work of local architects (very few of whom were trained outside of Louisville) be continually contrasted to, or regarded as a paler reflection of, the work of more famous architects in New York and Chicago. To attempt to squeeze local designers into a specific cubbyhole in the broader spectrum of American architecture is only to lessen their achievement, which, if judged in the light of Old Louisville, is considerable.

Given the growth patterns of Old Louisville, with blocks developing stylistically as the city expanded, and the uniform size and shape of the lots, many of the houses are basically the same repeated design, but each has been made unique by decoration. It is the ornamental details that make Old Louisville such a rewarding visual experience. Whether one wishes to find a reference to the Alhambrah in a Moorish doorway, or just enjoy its leafy interlacing, the total aesthetic effect is still the same. Terra-cotta arabesques, whimsical faces, cast-iron railings, cornice brackets, patterned brickwork, limestone lintels, columned porches, or the infinitely varied pieces of sidewalk sculpture—these are the monuments to the creativity of Old Louisville's architects, builders, and homeowners. The buildings along Third Street from St. Catherine to the University of Louisville provide one of the richest architectural experiences in the entire United States.

In time, Old Louisville may become, like Beacon Hill in Boston, Georegtown in Washington, and Society Hill in Philadelphia, one of the most desirable residential areas of the city. The great magnet of Old Louisville is its architecture. And, unlike Williamsburg and other village restorations, Old Louisville is not a museum with freeze-dried monuments, but a living textbook of three-quarters of a century of the city's history.

1435 Third St., 1961

Opposite: J. G. McCulloch's *ca.* 1897 house at 1435 Third St. is made of pressed or Roman brick. It is an early example of the revival of Georgian forms, such as the Palladian window, the hipped roof with balustrade, and the flat facade with emphasis on symmetry and horizontality.

The Victorian Scene

Architecture

The Courier-Journal, March 19, 1887

The home is an essential feature of Louisville, which has often been described as "a city of beautiful homes." There is no city in the Union where the domestic relations of the people are more charming than they are here. Strangers, as well as those native to the place, are affected by this fact and very quickly assimilate with their social surroundings. Other cities maintain more "style" in their homes; one finds more pretension and display in the houses of the Northern and Eastern cities of the size of Louisville; but nowhere does one find more comfortable houses, more ready hospitality, more generous living, or a more thorough air of ease, quiet and luxurious comfort than in the dwelling places of Louisville. One does not have even to enter the houses to discover the fact. It is made apparent in their very surroundings. There is an invitation in the ample lawns and cheerful fronts that stretch for miles along the streets of the city. Louisville covers a great amount of ground space. Its residents have never stinted themselves for room. The city has spread broadly over the large and level tract of country lying south of the river. Portland, Shippingport and Louisville were three villages that dotted the river bank. They were soon united into a municipality by the common interest people have who dwell near together. Then the town spread east, then south. A few years ago Parkland, the Homestead, and other neighborhoods were built up southwest of the city. A little later, people discovered that the most beautiful building sites for suburban residences lay east of the city, and the Highlands became popular. Later still the city was pushed farther out, and Clifton and Crescent Hill—both beyond the city limits—grew to be important suburbs of Louisville.

Nevertheless, the city's growth has been mainly to the south; the readiness of approach in that direction outweighing the fact that the land was flat and uninteresting. The growth has been steady since the Exposition of 1883 first brought a public into the neighborhood. Land has increased in value and many new houses have been built, on Second, Third, Fourth and Fifth streets, having especially shown the signs of progress

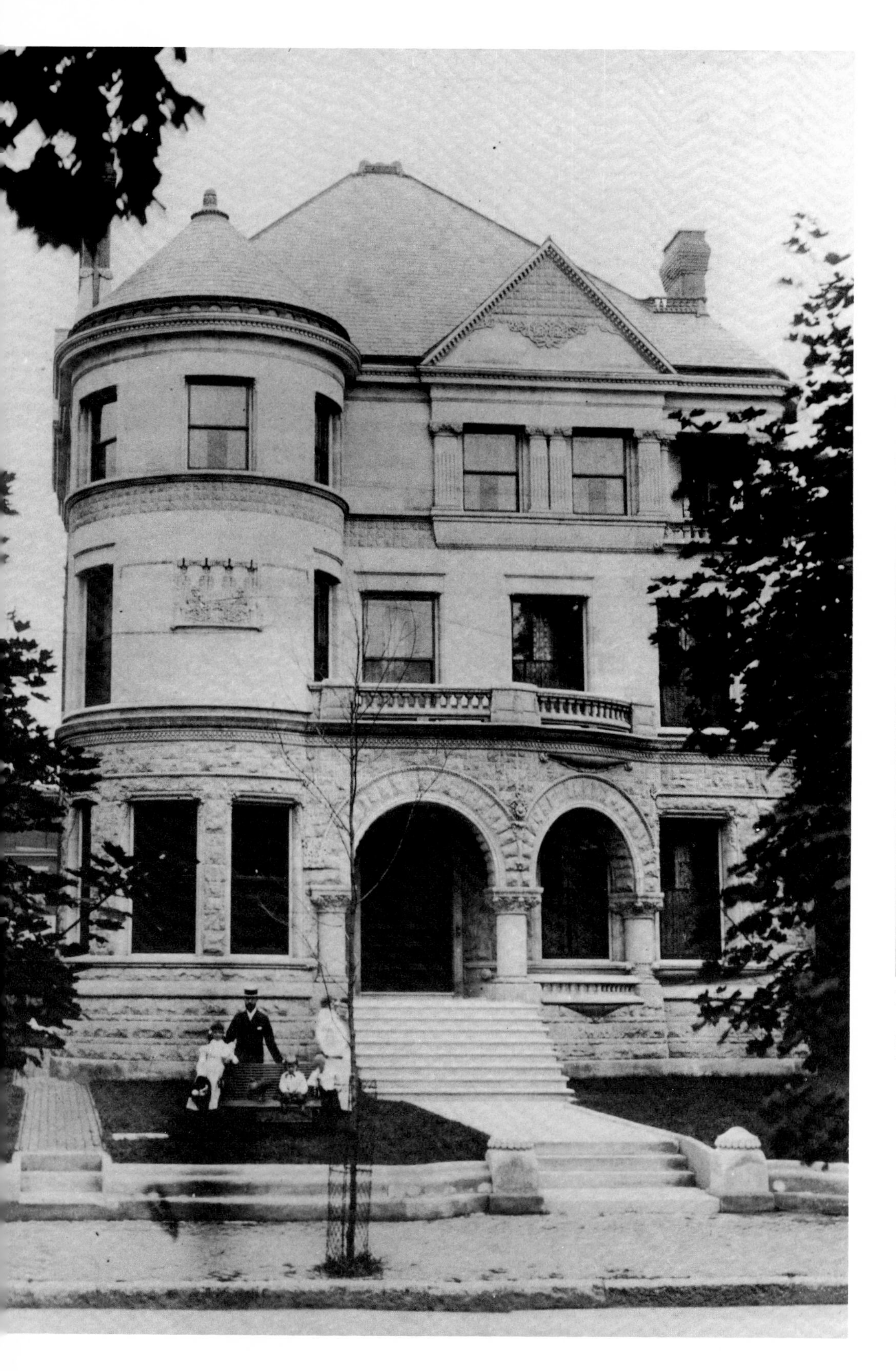

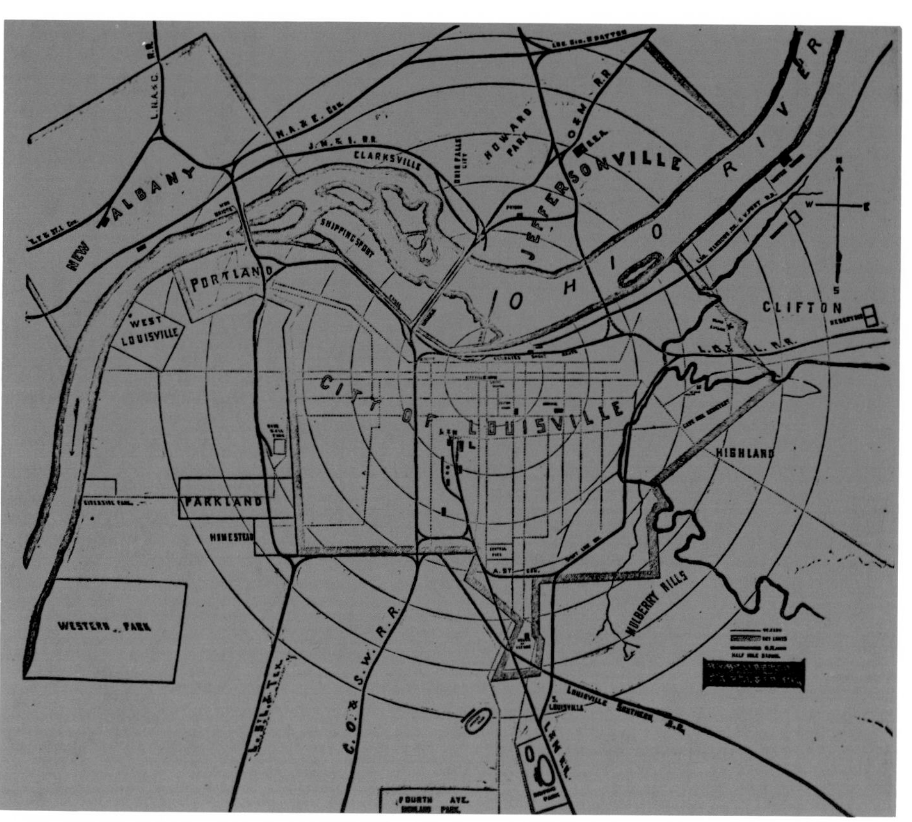

Left: The George A. Robinson House, 1015 Fourth St. about 1900. Above: Street and suburban railway facilities. *The Courier-Journal*, 19 March 1887.

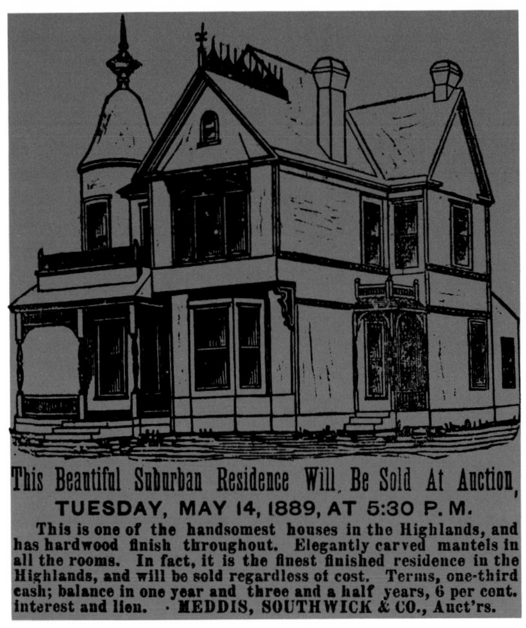

Above: The George M. Crawford House, 2744 Virginia Ave., Parkland, 1889. Left: Residence on Hepburn Ave. Demolished. *The Courier-Journal*, 12 May 1889.

and prosperity. The character of the architecture has improved, one might almost say, with each new building. The rapid development of Louisville, and even of Kentucky, is nowhere better illustrated than in the progress made in the architecture of the city. When one remembers that a hundred years ago a log house was a very good and respectable establishment in Louisville, and contrasts this with the elaborate detail and beautiful art of some modern residences and understands how absolute is the change that in a century has come in the manner of life of a Kentuckian.

In the collection of Col. R. T. Durrett are many pictures—rough drawings, most of them—which preserve the character of the early houses of Louisville. Col. Durrett has kindly consented to allow The Courier-Journal's artist to copy as many of these as are necessary to show the development of the city.

The first store in Louisville stood on the north side of Main street, between Fifth and Sixth. It was built by Daniel Broadhead, the first merchant, in 1783. Figure 1 shows this modest establishment, and points to the fact that in this early day the swinging sign was not an obstruction in Louisville. The store was a frame structure.

When one contrasts the vast expanse of buildings put up a few years since by the Newcomb-Buchanan Company—the largest distillery in the world, covering many acres of ground—with the little log-house shown in figure 2, which was the birthplace of the vast "whisky interest" one sees how small beginnings make great endings. Figure 2 is a picture of Louisville's first distillery. It stood at the foot of Fifth street, on the river bank, and was built by Evan Williams, in 1786. One year later Mr. William Johnston built the pretentious dwelling-house shown in figure 3, on the southeast corner of Third and Main streets. Mr. Johnston was Clerk of the County Court, and his house, though made of logs, was quite as good as that of his neighbors.

It was not until 1789 that a brick house made its appearance in the little city. It was built by Augustus Kaye, on the south side of Market street, between Fifth and Sixth streets. The house is shown in Figure 4. About the year 1800 Capt. James Patten built a stone dwelling-house—the first in Louis-

First Court-House.

Second Court-House.

Third Court-House.

Fig. 4—First Brick House.

Fig. 5—First Stone House.

Fig. 1—First Store.

Fig. 2—First Distillery.

Fig. 6—First Printing-Office.

First Methodist Church

First Catholic Church.

Old Christ Church.

The Courier-Journal, 19 March 1887.

The United States Post Office and Customs House erected between 1885 and 1889 on the northeast corner of Fourth and Chestnut streets. Some plans were prepared by D. X. Murphy locally in conjunction with M. E. Bell of Washington. The construction was supervised by McDonald Brothers. Demolished in 1942, it is the site of the J. C. Penney Co., W. T. Grant Co., and the Walgreen Co. *Harper's Weekly Supplement*, 7 January 1888.

Opposite top: The College Street Presbyterian Church near Second St. was one of the earliest (1866-1867) erected in Old Louisville. The chapel's unpretentious Renaissance Revival design was by John Stirewalt. Bottom: The Gwathmey-Grayson House (*ca.* 1810) shown in 1954 with Victorian alterations, was demolished two years later to make way for the State Office Building at Sixth and Cedar streets.

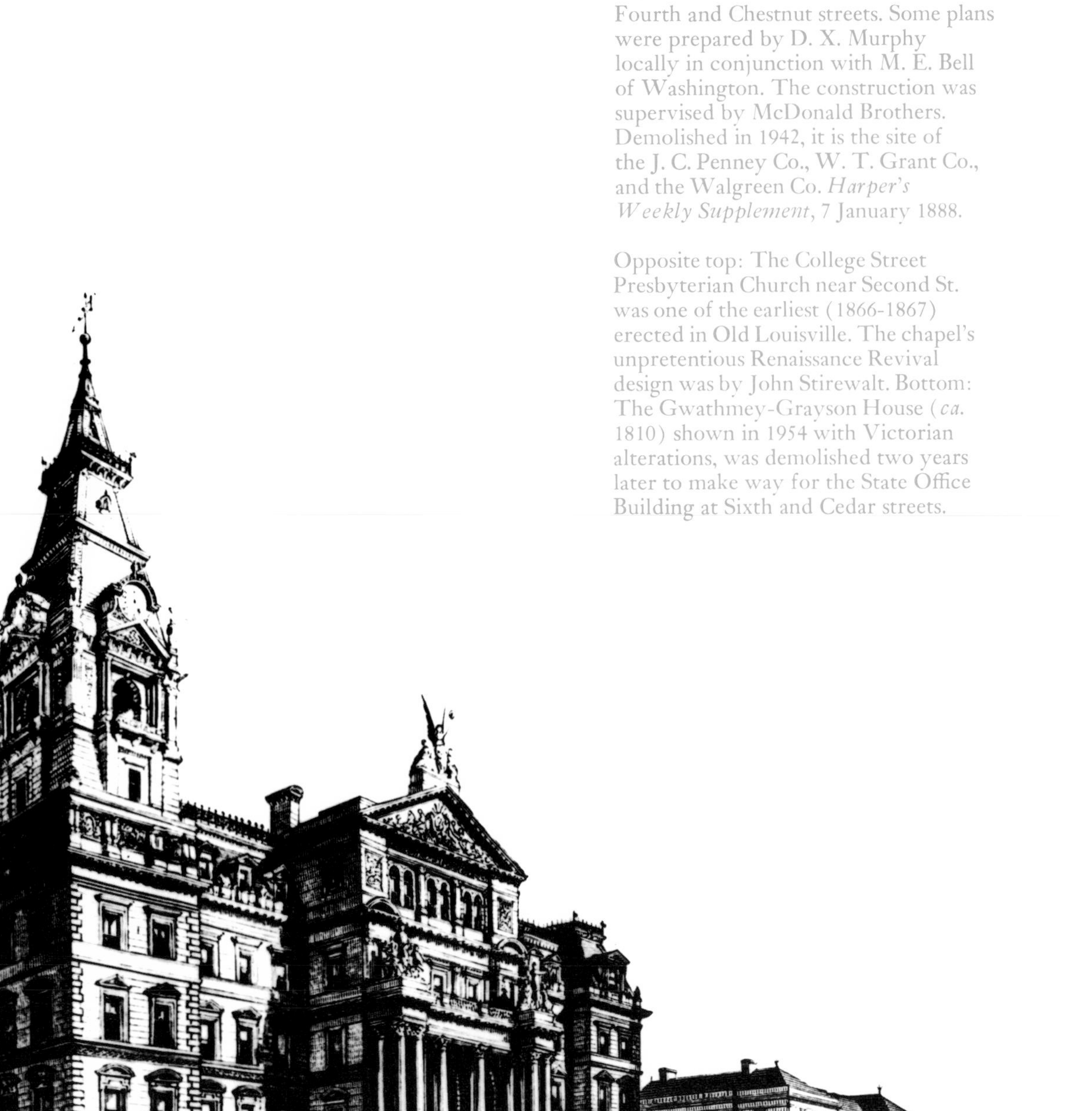

ville—on the square bounded by Main, Eighth and Ninth streets and the river. Figure 5 shows this dwelling.

No printing office had yet made its appearance here. One was built in 1801, near the northwest corner of Main and Sixth streets. It was from this office, figure 6, that Samuel Vail issued the *Farmer's Library*, a weekly paper that was Louisville's first journal. The house was made of logs.

Louisville now takes some pride in her public buildings. The city hall is a handsome stone structure, elaborately ornamented, with carvings in relief. Its proportions are graceful and elegant. The county court-house is a very fine specimen of the architecture of the Grecian temple, its noble portico and columns being worthy of admiration. The Government building now building will be one of the handsomest in the country, its estimated cost being $2,000,000. The first courthouse in Louisville was built in 1785. It is shown in an accompanying illustration. It was built of logs, was sixteen feet square, with a clapboard roof. The small building adjoining was the jury-room. It was twelve feet square. This building was destroyed by fire in 1787. In the following year the second courthouse was built. It was of stone, square and ugly. In 1811 the third court-house, built of brick, was erected. It seems to have been the first attempt at architectural adornment. It stood until the demands of the city necessitated a larger building.

About the first churches there was as little pretension to beauty as about the other buildings. The first Roman Catholic church was built of brick. It was erected on the west side of Tenth street, near Main, in 1811-12. The Methodists had a frame church earlier than this; but their first brick structure was built in 1812. It stood on the north side of Market street, between Seventh and Eighth. The first Episcopal church was Christ Church built in 1825 on its present site, Second street, between Walnut and Green. It has been twice rebuilt since it looked as the accompanying cut shows the building.

One of the oldest houses now standing in Louisville is what is known as the Grayson residence. It represents a style of architecture that prevailed in the second quarter of this century. The house is located on the west side of Sixth street, a few doors

north of Walnut street. The cut shown with this article is from a photograph taken a few days ago. The house appears just as it looked when originally built, and when there was little magnificence in the homes of Louisville. Not until years afterwards did the grand houses begin to appear. One of the first of these is now Miss Hampton's school, on the south side of Walnut street, between Third and Fourth streets. It is known to this generation as the Coleman house, but before then was occupied by George Keats, a brother of the English poet. It is a big, gloomy, square structure, with a large portico and heavy columns above the ample basement. Formerly a large yard surrounded it, and there was something sinister about the blackened statuary and waterless fountains that remained to suggest a faded grandeur. A child might have had a superstitious fear of the place, even though he did not know that it was in the parlor of this house that a daughter of George Keats shot herself. It is only fair to the present occupants of the dwelling to say that under their care the place has entirely lost its denuded and gloomy aspect.

It was not until fashion had reached Broadway that any street became noted for its fine houses. Between First and Fifth streets on Broadway stand a number of noble houses, surrounded by large yards. The oldest of them are broad and square, massive-looking and imposing. Broad halls run through the center of the buildings, which have a character that is distinctly Southern. The old Newcomb house, now a school, the old Ford house, now the residence of the family of Dr. Norvin Green, the Wilder house, the Bridgeford house, Capt. Silas F. Miller's residence and the residence of the late A. D. Hunt are among the oldest of these mansions. In the days of their glory the Ford house and the Newcomb house were palaces, their interiors being even more elegant than their exteriors. Both sit in large yards, the ascent to Dr. Green's establishment being up a broad, paved walk and fine stairway. On the corner of Third street and Broadway now stands a more modern residence—that of Mr. J. M. Atherton—very distinctly shown in the illustration. It is of pressed brick, and is beautifully and expensively finished. On the block below are the residences of John B. Smith,

Opposite: Entrance to the Ford-Green Mansion, 206 W. Broadway, *ca.* 1890.

Left: Back porches on the Second St. side of the Ford-Green Mansion, *ca.* 1890. Right: Interior of the Ford-Green Mansion when used by the Y.W.C.A. *The Courier-Journal*, 6 April 1930. Below: The Horatio Dalton Newcomb House (*ca.* 1859) at 118 W. Broadway was also designed by Whitestone. In 1891 it became St. Xavier College, and after extensive modifications served as St. Xavier High School until it was demolished for Stouffer's Louisville Inn.

Opposite: The Peaslee-Farnsley House (*ca.* 1877), 1235 Third St., shown in 1889.

Top: Broadway east of Third St., *The Courier-Journal*, 19 March 1887. Houses from right to left were owned by: J. M. Atherton, G. W. Swearingen, and W. H. Dillingham. Bottom: Broadway east of Fourth St., *The Courier-Journal*, 19 March 1887. Houses from right to left were owned by: B. F. Avery, W. C. Hall, and A. D. Hunt.

Top: Salt agent John B. Smith built his residence on the southwest corner of Third and Broadway *ca.* 1864. Victorian details had been added when shown while owned by manufacturer J. S. Lithgow in 1889. Bottom: Dr. E. W. Standiford's home at 924 Fourth St., designed by Henry Whitestone, photographed just before being razed for an automobile dealership in 1959.

the late A. D. Hunt, the late B. F. Avery, and other wealthy men.

A style of architecture that prevailed in Louisville ten years ago, and that is still more or less used, is admirably shown in the picture of the house of Dr. E. D. Standiford, which is on Fourth street, between Breckinridge and Kentucky. Some five or six years ago occurred a very decided change in the domestic architecture of Louisville—a change that will be of vast benefit to the city. People began to want, not only expensive houses, but beautiful houses, and if they have not always succeeded in obtaining good results, at least their aspirations have been in the right direction, and the houses that have been built have had the desirable effect of varying the monotony of the architecture. One deplorable fault in the houses of this city is the building of a front of stone or pressed brick, while the sides, which are quite as much exposed to view as the front, are made of ordinary brick. The effect is that of an embroidered silk panel inserted in the skirt of a plain print dress. Too many of the new houses have preserved this evidence of bad taste; but it has fortunately been rebuked by a number of beautiful buildings, which, while perhaps more modest than their neighbors', are certainly more beautiful and more artistic.

The Queen Anne craze and the early English have struck Louisville very decidedly, and most of the new houses are in those styles; but the architects themselves do not seem to have a very keen appreciation of a pure style of architecture, and some ugly results are the consequence. Louisville has access to unlimited and varied building materials. Beautiful pressed bricks are made here. Near by are quarries of stone of several colors and easily wrought. Numerous kinds of wood are within easy access. Land is cheap in the city, and a handsome house is a comparatively inexpensive luxury. A very effective bit of French architecture is that of the residence of Mr. Peaslee, on Third street, shown in an accompanying cut. The front is of green stone—the natural color—and the sides are of brick, painted green.

One of the best of the Queen Annes is just built on Third street near the southern end of that handsome avenue.

Above: Queen Anne "tenements" on the northwest corner of Third and St. Catherine streets. *The Courier-Journal*, 19 March 1887. Right: The George H. Hoertz House, 1625 Third St., built *ca.* 1887. Demolished.

It belongs to George Hoertz. In the Highlands—East Broadway—are several pretty Queen Anne cottages, besides a number of handsome residences of an essentially modern style. On First, Second, Third, Fourth and Fifth streets, besides on a number of intersecting thoroughfares in the southern portion of the city, are beautiful new houses, some handsome and very expensive, others less costly. Landlords are building their tenements with a view to making them attractive to the eye. Of course, Fourth and Third streets are the handsomest avenues, most of the houses on these being occupied by their owners. A glance at the illustrations will show how varied are the styles of dwelling houses; but there is that about the streets of Louisville which can not be reproduced in newspaper illustrations. The broad, green lawns where the bluegrass is dotted with trees and clumps of flowers, the wide streets, the ample sidewalks, with their fringe of maple, linden, elm or oak—these things must be seen to be appreciated.

It must not be supposed that only the wealthy can afford to live in pretty houses. An illustration is given of a row of pretty little Queen Anne houses on St. Catherine street, which are rented for not more than plainer buildings bring. Many such houses have recently been built in all quarters of Louisville, and as taste improves they will be even more abundant.

In the business houses there has not been so great a change in the style of architecture. The business sections being already built up, new houses do not so frequently make their appearance there as they do in the outlying quarters of the city. Nevertheless, even here there has been a change and an improvement, and now a man who builds a business house in a close block makes some effort to adorn its front. The Mammoth Clothing House, on Market street, between Fourth and Fifth, is a handsome pressed brick building trimmed with tiling. It is but indifferently shown in the illustration. The Bull Block on Fifth and Market streets, is architecturally handsome, as well as large. The Courier-Journal Building is one of the largest as well as one of the handsomest structures in the city. It is of red brick, trimmed with stone; is five stories high, surmounted by a tower, and is altogether the handsomest newspaper building

The Courier-Journal Building, opened in 1876 on the southeast corner of Fourth and Liberty streets, is shown in 1895.

The recently demolished Kenyon Building is at the left; the Bull Block (replaced by the First National Tower) is in the center; and the second Galt House is at the right. Photograph taken from City Hall in 1889.

in the West or South. A business block that is just completed is the Kenyon building, on Fifth street, between Market and Main. It is of pressed brick and brown stone, and is the most elaborate in ornament and finish of any of the business houses of Louisville. For the most part the remainder of the large business houses are merely massive, commodious structures, typical of the character of the commerce and of the merchants of the city.

A building that will adorn the city is the Baptist Theological Seminary, to be built on Broadway, between Fourth and Fifth streets. It will be handsome and expensive, as shown in the illustration.

Building Operations

The Courier-Journal, March 19, 1887

The use of red sandstone for trimming residences of red brick is a comparatively new architectural fashion. It was introduced in the East three or four years ago, and its utility lies in the fact that it does not wash out under rains and stain the bricks, as white stone does; or, if it does, being about the color of the brick, the washing does not show. The red stones used were at first brought from Denver and the Lake Superior region, but some months ago a quarry of it was discovered near Kyana, in Indiana, on the Air Line road, not far from Louisville, and being cheaper from the shorter distance required for transportation, has taken the place of the other. The stone, when carved and smoothed, has very much the appearance of terra-cotta, and there are few residences now going up in Louisville in which it is not used.

One of the most convincing proofs of the business advancement of Louisville is in the number of beautiful residences planned for erection the ensuing summer. Handsome residences always follow the accumulation of fortunes, and their number is a sure index of a city's financial condition. Among those to be built the following are a few of the most notable reported by builders:

Foster Thomas, President of the Kentucky Flour Company, a pressed brick, on Fourth street, near Weissinger avenue, to cost about $20,000.

1322 Fourth St., 1961.

Above: The extensively remodeled (*ca.* 1880) library of the White-Carley House (*ca.* 1869) at 835 Fourth St. President Arthur was entertained here in 1883. Right: Hall in the White-Carley residence shown in 1880.

Chas. Johnson, of Von Borries & Co., will erect a tasteful house of pressed brick, with red stone finish, on Brook street, near Caldwell, at a cost of $6,000.

Mrs. C. K. Crawford is building a handsome three-story residence on Third, near Kentucky, at a cost of about $10,000.

Archer Harman has plans drawn for a beautiful house on Third and Weissinger avenue, which will cost $6,000. It will be of the fashionable red brick and sandstone.

Dr. Grant will build a somewhat similar one at the corner of Chestnut and Twenty-second streets, to cost $6,500.

Mrs. Bennett H. Young is to remodel her handsome residence on Fourth street and convert it into a double house.

A Home Paradise

The Courier-Journal, March 19, 1887

There is no other city in the United States which can show the wonderful growth in population that Louisville has enjoyed since 1880. The increase from 123,000 in 1880 to nearly 200,000 in 1887 reads like one of the miracles that happen in the West, where the sun sometimes sets upon an open prairie and rises upon a prosperous town. Estimated by the methods usually adopted for obtaining the population of cities, Louisville has now 200,000 and over, but the most careful and conservative of all the estimates, based upon the census, has been taken for safety, and that places the population at over 180,000. In seven years a new city of 60,000 has been added to the Louisville of 1880. To accommodate them the increase of business as shown in the bank clearings has been from $149,587,212 in 1880 to $233,311,327 in 1886. While the population has increased 45 per cent, business has increased 56 per cent. In that time four trunk railways have been added to the transportation facilities, and three others are in course of construction; from nine railroads in 1880 the list will be increased to sixteen in 1887. In addition to this the city is at the head of clear navigation on the Ohio, and enjoys the full benefits of river competition for freight in any direction in which trade can be carried.

A Jeffersonville, Madison and Indianapolis locomotive at Eleventh and Maple streets, *ca.* 1893.

Trees line Second St. south of Jacob, *ca.* 1893.

Opposite top: Peter-Burghard Stone Co., *ca.* 1897. Bottom: Hammock in side yard of Verhoeff House, *ca.* 1893.

The paramount reason for so great an increase in population is the marvelous healthfulness and beauty of the city as a place of residence and the unusual advantages it offers to all classes of people. The death-rate in Louisville previous to 1885 was 17.4 per 1,000, the lowest of any city of her class in this country, if not in the world. In 1886 it decreased to 15 per 1,000, a fall that puts Louisville upon a health footing with the small town, where there is always so much pure air and so little danger from overcrowding that health is at its highest premium.

The healthfulness of Louisville is largely due to the fact that there is less crowding of the population here than in any other city in the country. Louisville covers almost as much territory as New York city, and is almost as conveniently supplied with means of city and suburban transportation. In Cincinnati residence houses will average five to each one hundred feet, while in Louisville the average is but little more than two to the one hundred feet, if that much. Every house here has its yard, whether it be the palace of a millionaire or the cottage of a laborer. So liberal has been the ground plan of the town that every man who is able to own a house is able to own his yard where the grass grows, the trees cast a grateful shade in summer, and where he can double or treble the size of his residence if he pleases. Instead of centralizing, Louisville has grown along the river and back over the healthful plain toward the splendid hills that cluster around at a short distance. Even on the Highlands above town, where so many handsome places are being erected, the same liberal provision is made. In such a city parks, as "breathing places," are almost unnecessary. The whole of Louisville is one beautiful park in spring and summer, the streets shaded by trees, the yards verdant with turf and blooming with flowers. With streets broader than any other city save Washington, all of them paved and graded, with an abundance of clear and pure water, it would be a marvel if Louisville were not the healthiest place in the whole list of cities. With 144 miles of paved streets there are ninety-four miles of street railway, twenty-two miles of steam suburban railways, three miles of elevated railroad, 130 miles of water-mains which furnished in 1880, 2,304,039,675 gallons of pure water, and in 1887 3,540,-

Above: Fourth St. cars to Central Park, *ca*. 1890. Left: Daisy Elevated Railway Station, 1887.

907,125 gallons. The gas supply is equally extensive. The street and suburban railways carried last year 20,697,000 persons, at an average fare of less than five cents. This reads like a description of a Utopian city, and that is about what Louisville is as a place of residence. Every person within reach of these local transit roads averaged 100 rides during the year. With such splendid distances, pure air, pure water, multiplied advantages of convenience and comfort it is no wonder that the Louisvillian lives twenty-one years after life's active struggle is over.

The cost of homes in Louisville is comparatively less than in any other of the cities of her class, because real estate is so cheap. The city stands upon an elevated plain, seventy feet above the ordinary stage of water in the river, and which extends several miles in every direction beyond her present corporate limits and assures abundant room for expansion for many years to come. Excellent residence ground has been purchased on the lines of the street railways at from $5 to $8 per front foot. It has always been the policy to extend the streets to prevent overcrowding, and maintain Louisville's pre-eminence as a healthy and cheap-home city. The railroad system has culminated in a belt-line, which will, of course, mark the sites for manufactories, and the residence portion can develop as it pleases.

One of the most important features of any city, as a place of residence, is the completeness of its public school system, where children are educated most effectively at the least expense. In this respect Louisville is quite up to any city. It has already thirty-five handsome public school buildings, where 16,926 pupils are in attendance, and who are taught by 404 teachers. The expenditure for education in 1885-6 was $313,-571.56, and the system has never exceeded its income but one year, when there was a pressing demand for new buildings. The Male and Female High Schools (separate) are very handsome institutions, where a full collegiate course is taught. In addition to the public schools, some of the most celebrated private seminaries in the West are located here. There are four medical colleges, two theological schools, one law school, a pharmaceutical college, and the public library, which contains 40,000

The Female High School completed in 1873 could accommodate 600 students. Now incorporated into Ahrens Vocational Technical High School, it is shown in a deteriorated photograph about 1890.

Above: Pupils of the Third Ward School on Broadway between Clay and Shelby streets, 1887. Left: Football game for the championship of the South held at Fountain Ferry Park won by Virginia over Vanderbilt. *The Courier-Journal*, 13 November 1898.

volumes of the most valuable reference and current books. It would be difficult to find a city where the educational advantages were more varied and extensive. The system of teaching beginners in the public school is an improvement upon that known in any prevailing system, and little ones are taught to read and spell more rapidly than anywhere else. A good ordinary education can be obtained by a child in from six to eight years. The school age embraces all children from six to twenty years of age, and the night schools, which are conducted every winter, have practically no limit as to age, so that anybody may secure a free education.

The provisions made for public charities upon a magnificent scale, is, perhaps, the natural outgrowth of a sentiment founded upon a perfect home-life. The hospitals, asylums, homes and houses of refuge and reform in Louisville are so numerous as to astonish the stranger. The City Hospital, which accommodates several hundred patients, is one of the most imposing and beautiful buildings in the city, and, together with St. John's Eruptive Hospital, is free to all indigent persons. The United States Marine Hospital, conducted by the Federal authorities, is for the use of marine sufferers, and St. Mary and Elizabeth Hospital, the splendid charity of Shakespeare Caldwell, admits fifteen free patients suffering from railway accidents, and has six public wards for the poor. The Alms-house building, on the Seventh-street road, cost the city $210,000, and is supplied with a full medical board. Besides these the University School of Medicine, and the Hospital College of Medicine, conduct free dispensatories, as do the homeopathic physicians. The Masonic Widows' and Orphans' Home is one of the most interesting institutions in the State, and is the only one of its kind in the world. An immense and handsome structure it is, dedicated as a home for destitute widows and orphans of Kentucky Masons, and an infirmary for the reception of sick and afflicted Free Masons. It is free from debt, and annually the whole people of Louisville take a holiday and contribute to the fund to sustain and promote it. The Louisville Houses of Refuge for white and colored children are celebrated all over the country. They are situated in the outskirts of the city, in the midst of beautiful

Masonic Widows' and Orphans' Home, on the east side of Second St. between Bloom and Avery, was opened in 1871 but not finished until 1881.

The Confederate Monument, shown in 1906, was erected on Third St. in 1895. At the right is the main building of the House of Refuge (campus of the University of Louisville), designed by Henry Whitestone and now the site of the J. B. Speed Art Museum.

Opposite: Norton Memorial Infirmary (*ca.* 1889) on the northeast corner of Third and Oak streets, 1897.

grounds, and have cost about $175,000. Boys and girls are not sent there as to a penitentiary, but are educated at schools regularly maintained, and taught honest trades. The city owns a work-house for her prisoners, which has its own means of support, and cost about $250,000. There is certainly no city in the United States of like size where the public buildings dedicated to charity and reformation are so splendid and varied.

The charitable institutions that have been mentioned are owned and controlled by the city or are partially public. There are many private institutions that would swell the list immeasurably. The Kentucky Institution for the Education of the Blind is a fine establishment, situated in the suburbs, and has a printing-house for the blind attached, to which the Government has made appropriations. This is one of the most singular as it is one of the best-managed institutions in the world, where scores of blind children are educated and made self-sustaining in many instances. The Morton Church Home and Infirmary, endowed by Mr. John P. Morton, who gave $100,000 for the purpose, and the John N. Norton Memorial Infirmary, endowed by the late Rev. John N. Norton, are institutions that would command admiration in any city in the world. They are to some extent private asylums for the sick and suffering, and are both conducted by the Episcopal churches. St. Joseph's Infirmary is widely known, while the Home of the Innocents, the Home of the Friendless, many orphanages, and fourteen convents and asylums conducted by the Catholic churches, make up such a list of charitable and cheap provision for the sick and destitute as no other city in the world can match. Louisville ought to be called the City of Magnificent Charities.

The Exposition of '87

The Courier-Journal, March 19, 1887

At the time this edition of The Courier-Journal goes to press arrangements are progressing for holding the great Exposition in Louisville this year in the grounds and buildings of the Southern Exposition Company. These Exposition buildings were erected in 1883 for the great Louisville Exposition of that year.

"The Louisville Exposition—Reception of Official Visitors—Drawn by H. F. Farney." *Harper's Weekly*, 4 August 1883.

The Courier-Journal.

VOLUME LXV. LOUISVILLE, THURSDAY, AUGUST 2, 1883.—SIXTEEN PAGES. NEW SERIES, NO. 5,328.

THE GREAT SOUTHERN EXPOSITION!

THROWS ITS DOORS OPEN TO THE WORLD.

A VIEW OF THE MAGNIFICENT BUILDING.

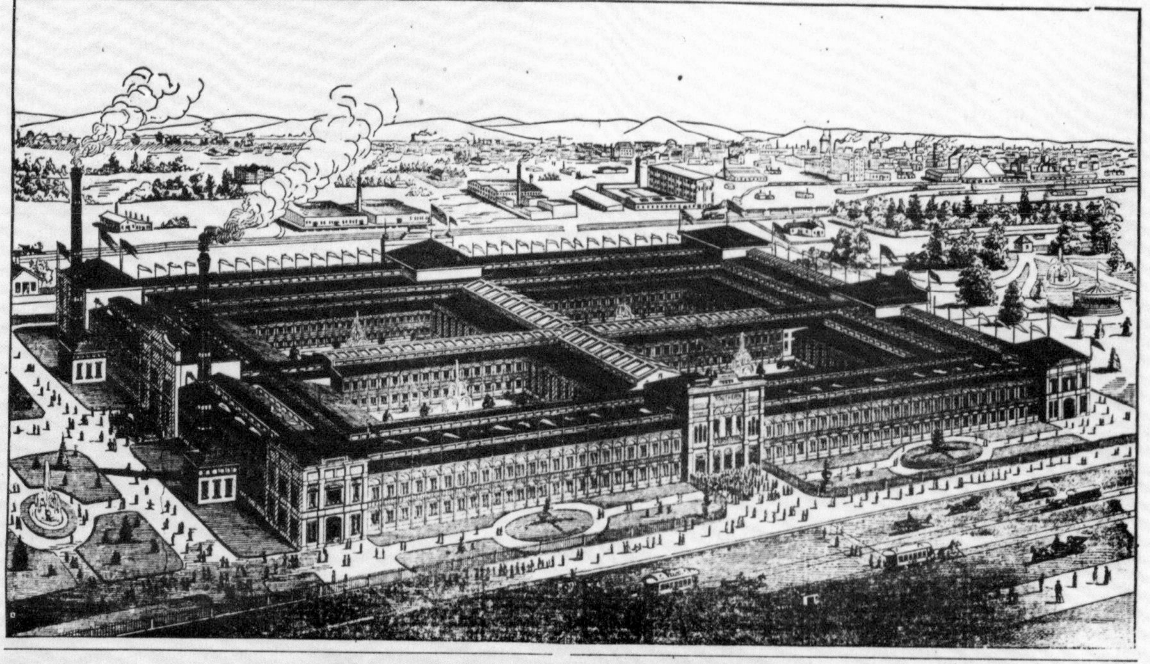

A PLAN OF THE GROUND FLOOR,

Showing Accurately the Location of All the Various Departments, the Machinery, the Annex, the Farm, the Flower Garden, Etc.

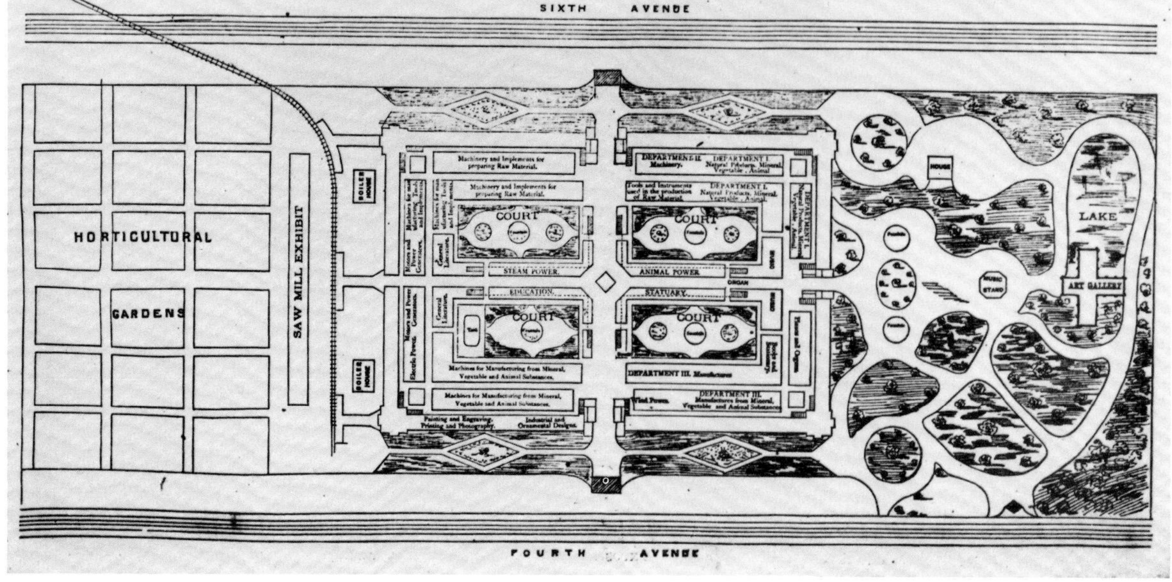

The grounds are situated on Fourth street, the most beautiful avenue of the city, and about fifteen minutes' ride from Main street, the principal business thoroughfare. The grounds are handsomely laid out, and are accessible by several street-car lines from all parts of the city. The main building has about eleven acres under roof, a railroad switch to its freight-receiving platforms and every other convenience. While the Exposition Board has not yet made final announcement of the proposed Exposition the necessary preliminary arrangements are every day making progress toward completion. The Exposition will probably be held from August 27 to October 22. The contemplated arrangements and the general idea now under discussion of details are indicated in what follows:

The Southern Exposition at Louisville will be of particular interest this year because of the great attention now given to the South, and its being the only exhibition connected in any way with the marvelous development of that region. When it is opened to visitors in August for its term of eight weeks, it is expected it will be an illustration of what is known as the new South. The excellence of its features of entertainment is well known to the whole country. While maintaining this degree of excellence, the purpose is to make its special attractions of an entirely novel and popular character. It will be a representative Industrial Exposition, and a place of popular amusements, that in quantity, quality and cheapness of admission will not be excelled anywhere in the world. The hundreds of thousands of visitors who have been familiar with the past exhibition may expect to find the Southern Exposition of 1887 entirely new in all its features. A general invitation is extended to the whole South to exhibit here everything it can produce, and the people of the whole country are invited to come here to witness this epitome of the new Southern development. The great advantages which the Southern Exposition offers are well known to exhibiters from other parts of the United States and many countries in Europe, and they have the assurance of the past that they will be welcomed. The fact that manufacturing exhibiters have always been so successful in selling and taking orders is an assurance that they will be represented in the ap-

"The Louisville Exposition—The Opening Ceremonies—Drawn by H. F. Farney." *Harper's Weekly*, 4 August 1883.

Top: Mule car in front of the Southern Exposition, 1886. Bottom: Cottage erected by Swiss Colonists in Kentucky at the Southern Exposition, 1883.

proaching exhibition.

The recent rapid development of the South is undoubtedly the result of the Expositions held in this region. The Atlanta Exposition, the first in order, gave to the country some idea of the vast resources of the South, and the beginning of its industrial development. The magnificent displays at the larger Southern Exposition, at Louisville in 1883, was a revelation to the country and the visitors who came from abroad. Then came the World's Exposition at New Orleans, and its successor of the following year, and the several annual exhibitions of the Southern Exposition at Louisville, all of which kept alive and extended the newly-awakened interest in the South. It is safe to say that without these Expositions the wonderful era of prosperity now started in the South would have been postponed many years.

The Southern Exposition at Louisville will be the only exhibition in the South in 1887. It will be the only place within that region where Southern products and the possibilities of new Southern industries can be collectively displayed, and where visitors to the South can conveniently and at their leisure study them. With a full display of the vast and various resources that have so suddenly sprung into importance, presented in a satisfactory manner at the Southern Exposition, a knowledge of the new South will be gained by thousands of persons who could not conveniently visit all the places of interest in the Southern States. After examination of the display of Southern resources in the Exposition at Louisville, visitors from the North and from abroad will select the points of greatest interest in the extension of their trips. It will therefore be a matter of importance to every part of the South to be handsomely and fully represented in a display. The exhibit that attracts the most attention will most readily awaken interest in the particular section from which it comes, and direct visitors to its home locality. The Exposition will be open to the display of not only the natural products and the industries of the South, but to the exhibition and distribution of charts, maps and printed information, in attractively arranged spaces, showing the advantages of localities, lands and sites. In a word, every reasonable facility

Magnolia west of Fourth; St. James Court is on the left and Central Park on the right, 1903.

will be offered for the representation of every interest of the new South. As the flow of visitors toward the South will be stopped at Louisville to examine the Exposition it will be to the interest of every man in the South who has any thing to sell or any industry to meet these strangers here.

While the primary purpose of the Southern Exposition is to illustrate the advance of art, science and industry, and the progressive utilization of the natural resources of the country, its aim is also to offer its visitors special attractions and entertainments that will add amusement to its business and instructive feature. It contains an art gallery of ample dimensions, in which it is proposed this year, in addition to its collection of paintings, to present everything representative of the present condition of decorative art.

The Music Hall, opposite the Art Gallery, in the center of the building, is a well-arranged opera-house. About 3,000 people can be seated in the auditorium, and the stage is one of the largest and best-arranged in America.

It is proposed in this hall to present a succession of amusements and attractions of the very best character. Heretofore during the Exposition only instrumental concerts have been held in this hall, and it was found that, notwithstanding the high excellence of the music thus produced, there was a desire for some variation in the entertainment. To meet this demand, an effort will be made to secure a series of operatic and dramatic performances, concerts and other entertainments that will please the public.

For the purpose of enlivening the promenade of visitors through the building, it is proposed to have a band of music stationed in the center of the building, to play while visitors are moving about and while no performance is going on in the Music Hall.

The Exposition Company is also contemplating a grand opera festival during the last week in May, similar to the remarkably successful festival of that character held last spring. It is probable that the National Opera Company, with its famous singers, its chorus of one hundred, and its ballet of over eighty beautiful dancers, will give seven operas on a magnificent scale.

Top: Southern Exposition Art Gallery and lake in Central Park, *ca.* 1885. Bottom: Tennis in Central Park, 1907.

Opposite: DuPont Square, later called Central Park, 1897.

The performances of this opera company are of greater magnitude and splendor than any ever witnessed in America. At times more than three hundred persons are on the stage, surrounded by the most beautiful scenery that can be produced, while Theodore Thomas conducts the orchestra of sixty accomplished musicians. When the arrangements for the festival are completed the seats will at once be offered for sale on the diagram, and the experience of last year assures the fact that they will all be promptly purchased. It is worth remembering that when this event is announced those who do not promptly purchase seats will find it impossible to do so, except at second-hand and at advanced price.

The Buchanan Sale

The Courier-Journal, December 17, 1884

A big policeman stood at the door of No. 931 Fourth avenue yesterday and warned everybody who passed in to "keep your hands on your pocket-books." The entrance was to the palatine residence formerly occupied by the family of George C. Buchanan. The occasion was the trustee's sale, at public auction, of the costly furniture and fixtures.

The crowd that gathered was notable for its elegance, large numbers and many ladies. Fully 500 thronged the hallways, blocked the staircases, and filled the parlors and reception-rooms, but the majority were present to satisfy an idle curiosity. It was a luxury to gaze upon the magnificent appointments. Nothing short of the most lavish outlay of means could have provided such a bewildering array of blended utility and artistic beauty.

Even the coverings on the walls have been made the subject of aesthetic study. This was shown in the new wall-papers, frequently designed to imitate metal, leather, majolica, delft and porcelain tiles. The wall ornaments, such as paintings, frames, plaques and statuettes, were in perfect keeping. The floors were richly carpeted, and variety, beauty and a perfection of finish was everywhere visible in the handsome polished wood appointments arranged in sections of various colored boards, yellow satin wood, white ash, yellow maple, buff oak

Opposite: The Tompkins-Buchanan House can be seen at the left of the old Presentation Academy on the northeast corner of Fourth and Breckinridge streets, 1897. Designed by Whitestone, it was built for Joseph T. Tompkins about 1871. Distiller George C. Buchanan obtained it after Tompkins died in 1877, but he went broke and left town. The house is now incorporated into Spalding College.

Above: A calling suit and home gown. *The Courier-Journal*, 19 May 1889.

and dark walnut. Holstery tapestries, damask curtains and portiers harmoniously contrasted with the wood finishings and wall-coverings.

The wall-coverings were made by Hegan Brothers, and are said to be the most elaborate of any in the Southwest, the cost of this work alone having been over $14,000. The side walls are covered with French *delicante papeur* of elegant design, while the ceilings and friezes are particularly fine. The library is papered with red bronze, with broad, hand-painted frieze and ceiling to match. The side walls of the reception-room are in green and bronze foliage, and the ceiling is in embossed red velvet laid in gold and picked out in transparent colors. The side walls of the drawing-room are in solid embossed gold paper, and the ceiling is beautifully frescoed. The dining-room walls are made to represent old tapestry designs, with the ceiling paneled in black walnut moldings, brass rosettes and hand-painted ornaments. Taken as a whole, the decorations are something simply magnificent, and as a specimen of the decorator's art, reflect great credit on the Messrs. Hegan. The work attracted great attention from those present at the sale.

The crowd began to pour in before 9 o'clock. The hour and a half which intervened before the auctioneer commenced the sale was devoted to an inspection of the furniture and equipments. Back and side entrances were locked and policemen were stationed at convenient intervals through the building to see that nothing unpurchased and not paid for was removed. From the first floor to the third the visitors elbowed their way, stopping frequently to admire some striking article of ornate furniture or work of art.

An item which attracted more than passing notice was a group of 28 paintings, thirteen being the creations of Mr. Carl C. Brenner. Another noteworthy collection embraced 26 handsome and valuable etchings in brass, the work of the late John Williamson.

At 10:30 o'clock Auctioneer Sim Meddis erected himself on a table in the back parlor and commenced the sale. The auctioneer's outfit consisted of a huge pair of eye-glasses and a rolled gold watch chain. Mr. Meddis displayed a slight nervousness as he looked before him into an army of expectant faces. Almost every lady present wore diamonds and a sealskin sacque.

Among the bidders were: Mrs. R. A. Robinson, Mrs. John M. Robinson, Mrs. Garvin Bell, Mrs. Samuel B. Churchill, Mrs. Wesley Read, Miss Minnie Read, Mrs. Hampton Zane, Mrs. Henry McDowell, Mrs. Bland Ballard, Miss Walker, Mrs. Bonniecastle, Mr. M. Muldoon, Dr. and Mrs. E. D. Standiford, Mrs. Wm. Cornwall, Mrs. M. L. Clark, Mr. and Mrs. J. G. Coldeway, Mr. John Hancock, Mr. John DeWitt, Mr. and Mrs. Henry Heath, Mr. and Mrs. J. T. Gathright, Bishop T. U. Dudley, Rev. J. G. Minnegerode, Mrs. James Barbour, Mr. and Mrs. John H. Weller, Mr. C. Henry Dorn, Mrs. J. B. Alexander, Mr. Joseph Brown, Mr. and Mrs. Cochrane, Mr. Julius Winter, Mrs. Allen Houston, Mrs. F. D. Carley, Mr. and Mrs. William Bridgeford, Mr. and Mrs. Flyshaker, Mr. and Mrs. Goram, Mrs. Quigly, Mr. and Mrs. Dennis Miller, Mr. and Mrs. Muir Weissinger, Mr. and Mrs. Beckley, Miss Lettie Robinson, Judge William Lindsay, Miss Muir, Gov. and Mrs. Luke P. Blackburn, Mrs. R. H. Higgins, Mrs. W. C. Tyler, W. Chambers Tyler, Jr., Mr. John Stratton, Mrs. Hatton and Mrs. Eugene Elrod.

Just before the bidding began a sensation was created by the announcement that a lady had been robbed. Policeman Jacobs had a few minutes beforehand ejected two suspicious-looking characters from the residence. An investigation developed that the lady who had been robbed was Mrs. A. T. Smith of No. 636 Sixth street. The lady claimed that a pocket-book containing $15 and several valuable notes had been abstracted from the inside pocket of her cloak.

The bidding was not lively, but the prices realized were satisfactory, averaging about 40 per cent of the actual value of the original purchase money. It was amusing to note two diamond-decked ladies trying to outbid each other. Such sport was relished by no one so keenly as the auctioneer. He never missed an opportunity to excite the indignation of rival ladies, and make the winning bidder pay the highest price possible.

Drawing room of the Tompkins-Buchanan House.

How They Spend Sunday

The Courier-Journal, April 8, 1888

Sunday diversions are as varied as weekday occupations. The different classes of people that inhabit a large city like Louisville have many ways to choose from in which to pass their day of "rest." Among these are card-playing, beer-drinking, billiard and pool-playing, theater-going, swimming and fishing around the falls, base-ball playing, driving and, of course, reading. A little later on picnics and cheap excursions will attract their quota of Sunday pleasure-seekers, but at this season of the year they are without admirers. Just now the first five named are very much patronized, and this being the time when the various brewers issue their flowing twelve months old "bock" beer, tipping seems to be leading the other four in an easy canter.

The German citizen who drinks delights in seeking the seclusion of a friendly saloon and there, sitting hour after hour, he seeks the "delightful" state of bliss that comes of a long engagement with "bock." He generally begins his Sunday by reading over the morning papers in a hap-hazard sort of way and when he tires of this joins some fellow spirits in the good old Teutonic game of "penuckle." Sometimes he plays "sixty-six," "euchre," "seven oudt" or "freeze out," but the traditions of his ancestry haunt him and he generally prefers the game they played before him. Ten-pin rolling is not indulged in to anything like the extent in this city that it is in many others, but there are a few who delight in it, and they generally spend their Sundays in trying to make "spares," or turning a graceful ball from the edge to the "General" of a "cocked hat" trio.

The hoodlum and semi-hoodlum elements congregate around certain corners and in vacant houses, or on the commons, and "shoot oontz," or tell the tales of their adventures, real and imaginary, criminal and romantic. They delight in detailing to each other, between numerous trips with the "growler," how they "fooled de durn copper." At the approach of night they are generally pretty well mellowed and are ready for a grand finale to the day by going in clusters to some cheap variety theater. They live for a few hours enchanted by the mimic life

Opposite: Side yard of the Verhoeff House, *ca.* 1893.

Left: Front stoop of the Verhoeff House, *ca* 1893.

Top: "How 'Mein Herr' Spends Sunday," *The Courier-Journal*, 8 April 1888. Bottom: "The Way His Money Goes," *The Courier Journal*, 8 April 1888.

Opposite: Fourth St. looking north near intersection of Walnut, 1907.

of the stage. They "blow in" all that is left of what they earned or otherwise obtained during the week before, and depart in a partially or wholly intoxicated condition. The odds are about one to two that they raise a row before they get to the respective places they call home and have to face His Honor in the City Court next morning.

As yet swimming is not indulged in to the extent that it will be later, but already there may be seen groups along the islands' sandy shores and on the dams, big and little, black and white, men and boys of all the lower strain of society spend a part of their time in "ducking" each other, diving and racing. The swimmers are most frequently seen and in greater numbers on Sunday than any other day. As soon as the water gets warm enough, there is not a Sabbath day that one will not find hundreds of persons doing the Indiana stroke, the sailor-stroke, or keeping themselves above water by doing the "dog paddle."

Isaak Walton, too, has many disciples, and they most generally select Sunday as the day to do their angling. A great number of those who are ambitious of landing fine specimens of the finny tribes go to the outlying small streams and lakes, which are within easy reach of the city. But by far the larger number do not care to do to even the small expense these trips require. They take their poles and lines, a can of bait and a basket of lunch, and repair to the wharfboats or get out on the dam and sit hour after hour waiting for a bite. Sometimes they are successful and bring home a good big string of perch, bass or cats, but more frequently they bring home only the dampening result of the fabled lone fisherman whose luck is proverbial.

Those of the gentler sex are very much limited in the means at their disposal to pass their Sundays in a manner congenial to most of their dispositions. They nearly all attend church as a matter of duty, and walk demurely home with their little sisters or Sunday school pupils. Afterward they may take a stroll together, or with their admirers and suitors, and even be so lucky, if the gentleman possesses such a luxury, as to sit behind a fast-stepping trotter or pacer. The drive is and always has been very popular with both young ladies and young gentlemen, but as it is expensive, only those with means can indulge often.

Eschewing all the other ways and means of connecting the two business weeks, the studious man, he who is inclined to go through life in the most sensible manner, with a regard for the commands of the good book, begins his Sabbath by a chapter in the Bible or a glance over the Sabbath-school lesson. When he has given his conscience a lease of rest by conforming to his religious fragrant Havana between his teeth, and a bundle of papers and books before him, gives himself up to the pleasure they afford him.

Unlike a great many of her more wicked sisters, Louisville's Sunday amusements and diversions are not of a more than moderately wicked nature. In this city there is a commendable lack of the extremely degrading and vicious pleasures that are indulged in so greatly in most of the other large cities, especially Chicago and Cincinnati.

On Fourth Avenue

The Courier-Journal, April 20, 1889

The bright and beautiful afternoons of the spring have literally packed Fourth avenue with shoppers, sightseers, dudes and citizens generally.

Old residenters, and as in every large and healthy community, there are plenty of them in Louisville, never pass along the avenue when the crowds are dense and are surging back and forth, making locomotion difficult to any but a woman, without instituting comparisons. They remember Fourth avenue of the past. A man need not be very old to recall a far different Fourth avenue from that of now. Middle-aged men have a pleasant recollection of the fruit shop which used to be at the southwest corner of Fourth and Green. Many even remember the gingham dress of the old Italian shopkeeper and the pretty skirts, neat ankles and wavy locks of the young granddaughter who assisted her and proved such an attraction to those same old residenters when they were young men. In the rear of this fruit shop there these old residenters were wont to drink the foaming lager.

Then and for many years later Fourth avenue bore but little resemblance to the metropolitan thoroughfare, with the elbowing crowds and animated scenes of the present day.

Until within the past few years men were easily able to walk along Fourth avenue on balmy afternoons. Now such a thing is a feat but rarely accomplished, especially since the dry-goods stores have spring displays in the large show-windows. Fourth avenue is lined on both sides with shops of this kind, and every establishment makes a specialty of show-windows and dressgoods display. A woman can no more pass one of these windows without stopping and looking than she can refrain from occupying more than half the seat in a street-car. When one woman stops, every woman within accessible distance hastens to that shop-window. Thus the crowd is augmented rapidly, and at last so dense becomes the throng that the sidewalk is entirely blocked. A woman was never known to leave a window until everything and every price in it has been examined, although that examination is the twentieth she has made within the week. When the women crowd the sidewalk, poor man has to walk in the gutter, and this happpens fifty times a day. The artist has not exaggerated in the least the scene depicted here.

Another picture taken instantaneously by the artist is that of a man who has had enough imprecation and anathemas hurled upon him during the past week to fill a dictionary devoted to that character of the English language. This man is fat, which goes almost exclusively into breadth of beam, and twice a day he promenades from Fourth and Main out Fourth avenue to Harris' Museum. He is an actor, and he strolls slowly along the street with a lordly air, totally unconscious of the crowd of peope trying in their hurry to pass him. He never moves from right to left and never surrenders his right of way. Consequently there is always a jam in the rear of this lordly but selfish creature, and everybody has to walk behind him, or if they are not satisfied with the actor's leisurely gait, then they are compelled to walk out into the street, and after passing him again take to the sidewalk.

Opposite: "After the Matinee—A Typical Saturday Afternoon Scene in Louisville," *The Courier-Journal*, 6 November 1898.

Above: A library and Harris' Museum were housed in the Polytechnic Building on the east side of Fourth St. between Liberty and Walnut, *The Courier-Journal*, 19 March 1887.

The Courier-Journal, 15 December 1889.

Opposite: *The Courier-Journal*, 1 December 1889.

Christmas Presents

The Louisville Times, December 15, 1884

The shop-windows along Fourth avenue and other retail streets are in full bloom with a profusion of beautiful holiday goods. For the coming two weeks notion dealers will be given a profitable impetus. The year has been a close one, financially, but the 25th of December without the customary accompaniment of bountiful gifts would be as much of a reverse on the recognized order of things as a snow-storm in midsummer.

The rich and the poor, the high and the low, all expect something. Any trifle is acceptable. The dirty little guttersnipe finds just as much happiness in the possession of a simple "kazoo" and a package of firecrackers as the juvenile with wealthy parents does in a mustang pony or a gold watch and chain. The natty house-girl looks upon a new apron with as much pleasure as the rich young lady bestows upon a costly set of diamonds.

At this season of the year such a bewildering array of fancy articles is presented that the purchaser finds it a matter of difficulty to make a selection. The ordinary father has $100 which he has laid aside for Christmas. The average young man invests from $10 to $25 in a present for his best girl. Every young lady knows somebody she wants to remember with a substantial offering. School children pick up the infatuation and attack the paternal pocket-book for money to afford an exchange of courtesies among themselves.

Aside from this there is another and important way of expending Christmas funds. It is in the way of charity. Every city has its numerous asylums for the poor and incapacitated; receptacles for the wretched beings who know nothing of the joys of life. It is in these dismal abodes that the shining dollar of the humanitarian, unloading a Christmas gift in the shape of delicacies and warm raiments, fills countless hearts with gladness. There are hundreds of wealthy men and women in Louisville who subscribe a portion of their Christmas money each year to a dinner for the orphan, the outcast and the decrepit.

It is impossible to lay down rules for the purchase of

Christmas presents. The tastes of the intended recipient should be studied, and an inventory of the personal exchequer taken. Even then the purchase is in doubt. A reporter for The Times started out this morning to consult the taste of every one he met upon the subject of Christmas presents.

"I shall give my girl a silk umbrella with a silver handle, and her name stamped inside," said an attenuated young man who smokes cigarettes and can always be seen at the matinees. "I have already priced the article and know exactly how much it will set me back—$15."

"I shall present my girl with a picture of myself," said a vain young man. "It's impossible to play draw poker and buy costly presents the same season," he added, philosophically.

"My wife," said a newly-married man, with a flash of pride, "gets a gold watch and chain."

"I'll buy my mother a pair of slippers and my father a new dressing gown," were the words of a thoughtful young man, whose salary is $15 week.

A banker said: "My wife is to have a $1,000 check. The children will have all the candy, rattles and dolls they can carry."

"Sister wants a box of lace handkerchiefs, and I guess she must have them. They cost $10," said a tall young man, who is at present industriously engaged in trying to raise a mustache.

"I can think of nothing nicer to take home with me than a $25 writing desk," said a merchant. "It will be useful and ornamental."

A plush handkerchief-box costs $6, toilet sets range from $3 to $10, and silk hose are $5 a pair. Any of these will prove acceptable to a young man's best girl. Small articles of jewelry are always in taste, and a copy of a standard author is a suitable present for the cultured. A great many wives buy imported cigars for their husbands. A bottle of perfumery was never refused, and silk handkerchiefs are useful. A card case, a picture, some article of furniture, a load of coal or a barrel of potatoes—something to supply every want and fit every condition in life can be found in the market.

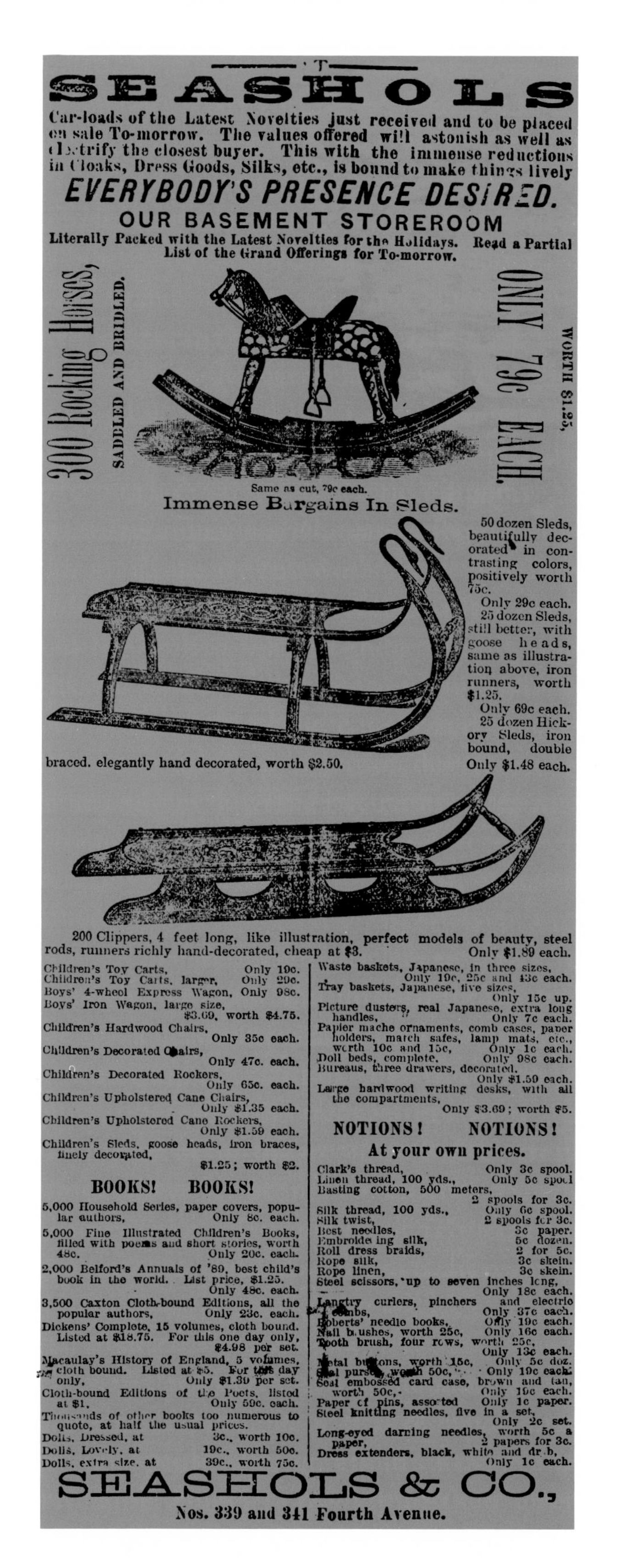

Life in a Tenement

The Courier-Journal, March 4, 1888

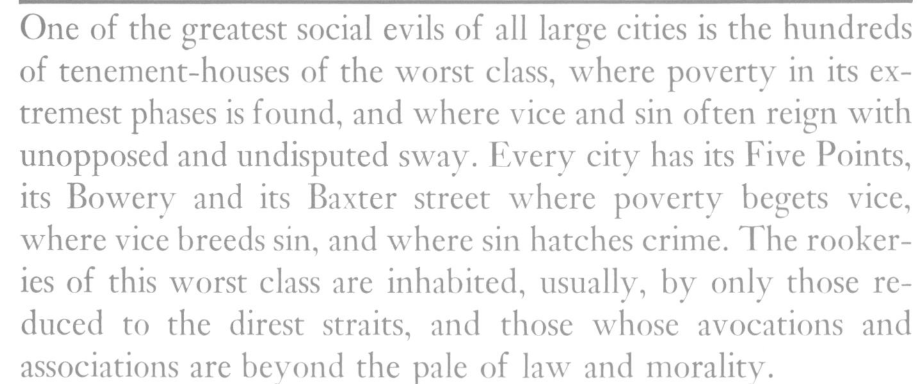

One of the greatest social evils of all large cities is the hundreds of tenement-houses of the worst class, where poverty in its extremest phases is found, and where vice and sin often reign with unopposed and undisputed sway. Every city has its Five Points, its Bowery and its Baxter street where poverty begets vice, where vice breeds sin, and where sin hatches crime. The rookeries of this worst class are inhabited, usually, by only those reduced to the direst straits, and those whose avocations and associations are beyond the pale of law and morality.

Louisville is not without a large number of tenement-houses of this class. They are scattered throughout the city, and can be found in all directions. Many of them are large buildings, formerly used for better purposes, and some of them are small ramshackle houses unfit for occupancy. In the larger ones dozens of families make their homes, and the smaller ones are also correspondingly crowded. Often a family of ten or twelve is found huddled in one or two small rooms, which are used as dwelling, sleeping and cooking apartments. The building, 119 East Market street, which was the scene of the recent Mary Gorman tragedy, is a tenement occupied by the most poverty-stricken and obscure classes, and life amid such surroundings must have much of bitterness and little of pleasure. The "Bee Hive," at Clay and Market streets; and Bowles Block, on Market street, between Floyd and Brook; the cottages in "Limerick," known as the "Twenty-one Row;" the old dilapidated frame building at Fifth and Kentucky streets, occupied by negroes; the large number of tenements about Clay and Main streets; those about the "Point" on the river front, many of those on Eleventh street between Main and the river, and a large number on the "Chute" and on the various streets near the river front, are over-crowded by those who are unable, and some unwilling, to make their homes in better quarters. In these houses ventilation and sanitary regulations are, of course, totally neglected, and the majority of them are the veriest pest-houses of disease and death.

Medical attention is too often the last mode of relief

Above: Wuersch's Saloon on the northeast corner of Twelfth and Maple streets, *ca.* 1894.

Opposite: Street children, *ca.* 1893.

resorted to in cases of sickness. The poor inhabitants are usually unable to pay for the services of a physician and medicine, and sickness in such a place is a living death. The extreme poverty and suffering of these people, too, begets a callousness that decreases the value placed upon human life, blunts the sensibilities and weakens ties of affection. The very nature of the life breeds disease, and children growing up in the foul and stifled atmosphere of these tenements are small, weak and unhealthy. Their lives are very hard, and the pleasures of childhood are but little known to them.

They are usually left at home, while their elders go out to work or to spend the time upon the street. The associations surrounding the children of poverty, who are often also children of sin, are the worst, and they soon become hardened and depraved. So large a number of the dwellers in these houses are of the worst class that the knowledge gained and the sights witnessed by the children are calculated to lead them to a life of sin and crime. Drunkenness and vice is constantly before their eyes, and even a worse degree of sin surrounds them. Women of the lowest class rent rooms in these buildings and use them for the most immoral purposes. A number of them are practically houses of prostitution, frequented by the worst characters.

A moral man, woman, or child living in these houses sees much to disgust and little to please. Should they prefer to make no acquaintances among those about them their lives are necessarily lonely, and if they make acquaintances they are found to be a disadvantage rather than a help. Often a poor woman will be in her room sick for several days without attention, and it is not infrequent that death comes to such, and finds them alone and unattended. Such of these women as are endeavoring to lead correct lives have but few acquaintances, and are almost friendless, and sickness never finds them prepared to meet it.

The lower classes of women who inhabit these houses are, perhaps, the most degraded. They ply their unlawful occupation openly, and continue to make many tenements very disreputable houses. They spend their days in sleep and recuperation and their nights in debauch and dissipated orgies. Their lives and actions lend an unsavory reputation to the scene of their habitations, and aid in making the tenement houses undesirable locations. Landlords of such property are careless about the persons to whom they rent, and as long as the rent is paid no questions are asked about the character of the tenants.

The saloons in the neighborhood are well patronized by the dwellers in tenements, and the favorite method is the pastime known as "rushing the growler." A nickel or a dime secures a pitcher or a bucket of beer, though a fried oyster or a hard-boiled egg does not accompany it and the family circle or the lonely inmate is accordingly solaced with the "flowing bowl" on a cheap scale. Drunken fathers spend their earnings for drink when their families are pinched by absolute want, and it is a matter of no surprise that their offspring follow in their footsteps.

The few honest and decent people living in tenements are their only redeeming feature, and their number is not large. Such people seek better quarters as soon as able, and find no congeniality among the class that inhabits the undesirable rookeries.

No better field for Christian work can be found than within the walls of these dilapidated and uninviting looking buildings. It was when there employed that the late Mrs. J. M. Sadd, of Sadd's Mission, did some of her most efficacious and noble work, and her name is yet revered by many who remember her deeds of charity and Christianity. To such as wish to labor in alleviating suffering and checking vice, their field offers opportunities for untold good, but it requires determination and courage to begin the work.

A Glimpse of the City

The Courier-Journal, September 6, 1888

The first thing that strikes the eye of the visitor accustomed to observation is the absence of the tenement house, while the multiplied numbers of comfortable cottages, each with its yard and garden, occupied by the working people, astonish him. A very large proportion of these are owned by those who occupy

Northwest corner of Fourth and Broadway, 1889. Houses from right to left were owned by: W. H. McKnight, Warren Henderson, and James Bridgeford.

THIRD PART. TWENTY-FOUR PAGES. PAGES 17 TO 24 INCLUSIVE.

The Courier-Journal.

THIRD PART. TWENTY-FOUR PAGES. PAGES 17 TO 24 INCLUSIVE.

VOLUME LXXIII. LOUISVILLE, THURSDAY MORNING, SEPTEMBER 6, 1888.—TWENTY-FOUR PAGES. NEW SERIES, NO. 7,190.

GROWTH OF A GIANT.

Historical Resume of the Growth of Louisville During Seven Years.

A City That Has Doubled Its Business and Its Enterprises In a Short Time.

What the Citizens Celebrate In the Great Industrial and Commercial Jubilee.

Features In Which the Falls City Leads All Others In the World In Enterprise.

CHARACTERISTIC TRADE LINES

In all the elements that go to make up a great and powerful city, Louisville is, beyond doubt, the chief metropolis of the Southern States. In the mere matter of population alone it was exceeded at the last census by New Orleans, but in

RESERVOIR, LOUISVILLE WATER-WORKS.

CITY HALL.

Third Ave. South from Oak St.

KENTUCKY INSTITUTION FOR THE EDUCATION OF THE BLIND—FRANKFORT AVENUE.

Fourth Ave. & Walnut St.

STORES ON MARKET STREET.

FEMALE HIGH SCHOOL.

W. S. MATHEWS' RESIDENCE. (Fourth avenue.)

UNIVERSITY OF LOUISVILLE—MEDICAL DEPARTMENT.

SIXTH AND MAIN STREETS.

A QUEEN ANNE. (Fourth avenue.)

MRS. E. F. AVERY'S RESIDENCE—FOURTH AVENUE AND BROADWAY.

STANDIFORD RESIDENCE. (Fourth avenue.)

HOLCOMBE MISSION.

A FOURTH STREET RESIDENCE.

The Courier-Journal, 6 September 1888.

them, and there is no reason why every industrious mechanic who comes to Louisville should not own a home of his own. Land offering little choice between a site for a palace or a cottage can be purchased more cheaply than in any other city of similar size in the country. Building materials are cheap, and living is at the lowest cost. The street-car system, which is the wonder of all who see it, renders distance a nullity. For five cents one can ride all over the city, and the system of free transfers makes it possible for householders to live in any section of the city they may choose.

As a residence city for all classes, Louisville enjoys many remarkable advantages, not the least of which is the taste which has been characteristic, from the first, in the beautifying and building of homes. The business quarter has always been plain—though the buildings have been equal to all the demands of an active commerce—while all who could build homes have made them as handsome as their means permitted. The great plain upon which the city was built, covering seventy square miles, and extending back six miles from the river to a group of picturesque "knobs" or hills, has afforded every facility for the economical gratification of taste. Ground being plentiful and level, distance was not difficult to overcome, and so, instead of being crowded into restricted limits set up by natural barriers, the city has spread at her own pleasure. The streets are broad, being fom sixty to 120 feet in width, all well drained, paved, and beautified with a profusion of fine shade trees. There are few cities in the world with such finely shaded streets as Louisville possesses, and none where the streets are wider. The residences are, as a rule, provided with spacious yards and gardens, and in the spring of the year a drive over the city past the miles of great yards, filled with flowers and shrubbery, and under the shade of trees rich with foliage and blossoms, is like a trip in fairyland. The average number of residences to the hundred feet in Eastern cities is about five; in Louisville it is about two. The favorite residence quarter for a number of years was south from Broadway, which divides the city parallel with the river. South Fourth, Third, Second, First, and Brook streets, are lined with lovely and costly houses in which the taste of the

In 1875, B. F. Guthrie purchased Herman Beckurt's House (*ca.* 1870) designed by Whitestone. Located on Third St. between York and Breckinridge, it was replaced by the Temple Adath Israel about 1907.

architect and the landscape gardener vie with each other for expression. Magnolia avenue, Kentucky, Oak, and St. Catherine streets, which intersect the others at right angles, are within this charming district, and present the same lovely spectacle. South of Broadway, and practically within the district outlined above, there were 260 residences built in 1885 at a cost of $1,600,000, or an average of $6,150 each.

Adepts with Rackets

The Courier-Journal, April 22, 1888

Tennis players, and the admirers of the game, were entertained yesterday afternoon, at the grounds of the Louisville Tennis Club, by a match game arranged between England and America, the former nation being represented by two visiting Englishmen, and the latter by two members of the Tennis Club. Messrs. Lee Robinson and George Norton played on the American side, and Messrs. Radcliffe and Burr on the English side. Mr. Radcliffe is well known to Louisville tennis players as an expert at the game, he having on several former occasions and with varying fortunes, contested with the best of the Louisville tennis enthusiasts. Mr. Burr's reputation as an adept with the racket lent great additional interest to the game. Mr. Norton and Mr. Robinson rank with the best of tennis amateurs, and great confidence was felt in their ability to cope successfully with the visitors. The umpires were Messrs. Christy Churchill and Sam Kenning.

It was agreed that the contest should be for three sets in five. At 3:30 o'clock the players took their positions, the Americans in and the Englishmen out, Mr. Norton doing the sending. The first ball fell gently in the half court guarded by Mr. Burr, and was immediately caught as it rebounded from the turf, and sent back over the net. Mr. Robinson caught it again and drove it back, to be again sent to the American side but with so much force that it passed the sending line, and counted the first fifteen points for the Louisville players. The next ball took the same course, and when driven back to the sending side, was met with a stroke which landed it against the net and made the score even. The play continued and

"Running For It," *The Courier-Journal*, 22 April 1888.

the home team counted up three more straight plays and won the first point.

The Englishmen did the sending for the second game, and counted up their plays rapidly, scoring "love 40" before the Americans had a chance to count. Then, just as Mr. Robinson made a clever stroke at a ball away off to the side, it flew wild, and gave the Englishmen the "love game." The play for the third point began by each side scoring fifteen.

The progress from this was even, and "deuce" was announced after a skillful play by Mr. Burr made the score 40 to 40. Mr. Norton sent the next ball over the net and let it drop gently in the half court, whence it was driven back to the American side to be again passed to the English side, and then over to the American side, where it dropped before either Mr. Norton or Mr. Robinson could reach it. "Vantage out" was the ruling of the umpires, but even with this in their favor the Englishmen were unable to win the game, and the score was 2 to 1 when the fourth game was begun, Mr. Radcliffe sending for the visitors side.

Mr. Norton's play was perfect in this, and the points were counted for the home team almost as rapidly as the ball could be sent over the net. The fifth game also fell to the Americans.

In the seventh, when the score was 30 to 30, the ball, just from Mr. Radcliffe's racket, was caught by Mr. Norton and sent back. It was again driven over the net, and then all four contestants engaged, and the prettiest and most skillfully played contest of the match followed. The light ball flew from racket to racket, and bounced in every direction so rapidly that it was hard to follow, but each time it was caught by one of the four, until Mr. Robinson finally slipped as he attempted to reach it when it was some distance from him. This permitted it to drop on the side of the net guarded by the home team and the Englishmen counted. The game and the next one were won by the Englishmen, and the ninth was then begun.

There was some clever playing in this by both Mr. Norton and Mr. Robinson, but the Englishmen again counted. The first set was completed after ten games, the score being six

"Sending," *The Courier-Journal*, 22 April 1888.

113 W. Ormsby, 1961.

to four in favor of the Louisville players.

The second set was distinguished by excellent playing by the Englishmen, but in spite of this, they were defeated by a score of six to five. The result might have been different, but for the fact that the visitors almost invariably struck too hard, and drove the balls beyond the sending or sidelines.

With the odds of two to nothing against them, there was but little hope for the Englishmen when the third set was begun, but notwithstanding, they played their best and hardest for the first two or three games. The Americans again had the best of it, and seeing the helplessness of their efforts, the visitors began to play carelessly. The result was that the third set also fell to the home team by a score of six to one, thus ending the game, the visitors having failed to win any set out of the three played.

The Building Outlook

The Courier-Journal, March 7, 1889

Louisville has better facilities than almost any other city that can be named but there is one serious drawback which operates to enhance the cost, which otherwise would be much less than in other cities, and that is the attitude of the Bricklayers' Union, of which much complaint is heard, not only among architects and builders, but among persons who contemplate investing. The number of knights of the trowel in Louisville is exceedingly small. They have steadily advanced wages until they now get $5 per day and have things pretty much in their own hands. They allow but few apprentices, so that there are not many accessions to the ranks of the journeymen, and recruits from abroad, also few, are either "persuaded" to get out of town or forced to become members of the union. The contractors are afraid to fight them and so are the architects. When the busy season sets in —and the outlook is now probably for the liveliest for years—there will be a great difficulty in obtaining men, even at $5 per day. This state of affairs will probably end in another advance in wages, and a consequent increase in the cost of building, unless some man or syndicate with ample capital shall take the bull by the horns, import workmen from abroad, and

Northwest corner of Fourth and Park,
1961.

so equalize the supply and demand. The builders complain, also, that all the workmen are placed on the same footing, and that when they do succeed in getting as many men as they need they are forced to pay inferior workmen as much as first-class ones.

The outlook for the present year is excellent. All the architects are busily engaged in drawing up plans and specifications for a large number of new houses of all descriptions, in addition to which there are a large number of large buildings talked of, which, as yet, have no existence except in the minds of their projectors.

In speaking of the outlook, the McDonald Brothers say:

1416 Third St., 1961

"Louisville has the best brick, sand, lime, and cement in the United States, and there is no place in this country where as good a quality of brick can be obtained. We are in a good situation as to lumber, and all kinds are cheap. We are situated between the white pine of the North and the yellow pine of the South, and have plenty of the best kind of poplar. If there was ever a good place to build, that place is here. Everybody is looking forward to increased business this year, and our present prospect is for an immense amount of work. A great many drawings are being made, but it is too early to speak of contracts —they will come later—but the outlook is splendid."

The House Beautiful

The Courier-Journal, January 28, 1900

The Queen Anne or Elizabethan "fad" or fashion for that style of dwelling house was the cause for a decade of years of a large number of attempts to reproduce this style. It permitted endless popular vagaries and few satisfactory houses of the period remain to-day. There is, however, one correct dwelling of the Queen Anne style on New Broadway. It was planned by Mr. Maury Mason for Mr. Charles Wood and is now the home of his widow. This gem is situated near the Highlands and is always greatly admired by all who see it.

Louisville has at present, a number of earnest workers in the architectural field, and the city, particularly the southern portion, shows their work better than words could tell it. Beau-

Left: "Modern 'Colonial' Residence," built *ca.* 1884 by Henry J. Tilford on the northeast corner of Fourth and Park. *Harper's Weekly Supplement*, 7 January 1888. Presently the site of an office building. Above: "A Pretty Queen Anne," on Fourth St. *Harper's Weekly Supplement*, 7 January 1888.

The W. G. Coldeway House, built *ca.* 1900 on the northwest corner of Third and Gaulbert streets, designed by Charles D. Meyer. *The Courier-Journal*, 28 January 1900.

tiful and practical houses line the streets and dot the open country, houses which give to the city her well-deserved title of the "City of Homes." The colonial fashion, revived some years ago, and immediately following the Queen Anne fad, has been largely replaced by the Italian Renaissance. This is following the Eastern fashion. Many of the houses built under the colonial influence, with the severity modified to suit the conditions of present life, are very beautiful and will never tire the public eye. One of the best examples of a colonial cottage in the city and one which has the highest artistic value as entirely suitable to the street and neighborhood in which it is built is the house of Mr. J. E. Whitney on the south side of Gray street, near Brook. This house is built on a fifty-foot lot and has many fine trees in the front grounds. The cottage is painted in lemon and white, has a fine porch, and all details about the doorway, etc., are carried out in true colonial fashion. The interior of this admirable dwelling is most homelike and artistic, and deserves special commendation in every respect.

The style of the hour, however, is the Italian Renaissance. Taken as a basis, it combines dignity and grace. Several of the Louisville architects have been most happy in combining the principles of this school with modern requirements. Since the World's Fair this style has been growing in favor, and now is the popular demand. Brick is the favorite material and of the Roman pattern. Bedford stone is the favorite for trimming, and solid stone porches are much in favor. There are few new fancy frame houses, and there are not many in prospect as the tendency of all builders is toward the more substantial edifices. The most of the architects expect 1900 to be a good year as the work now on hand promises well.

As the city pushes south and property becomes more valuable it is often necessary to design houses for narrow lots that shall yet be up to the demands of present life. Two of these are just completed at the corner of Third avenue and A street by Mr. William Coldeway from designs by Mr. Charles D. Meyer. The houses are built of pressed brick, with stone foundations and slate roofs. There are stone trimmings. They are ten-room houses with the reception hall as a special feature. This is finished with quartered oak, with a fine stairway and art glass effect. The houses seem very large and spacious although the two are on sixty-four feet of ground. Mr. Meyer considers them the best houses for small lots that he has built. The interior floors are inlaid in carpet effect. The cost was about $12,000 apiece.

The same architect has just designed a house for Mr. P. H. Holzheimer on East Broadway. The material is pressed brick front of Acme brick. The trimmings are of Lake Superior brown stone. The reception hall is in quartered oak, the other woodwork in hard pine. The reception hall is the special effect in this house. This house cost about $8,000.

Mr. M. Q. Wilson, the Main-street architect, gives a good design for a remodeled house fifty years old. This dwelling is the residence of Mrs. J. Moss Terry, and is located on Third avenue near B street.

Mr. J. J. Gaffney, the architect, has several very good modern houses on his list which may be tersely described as follows. John D. Taggart, Jr.'s country house—Fern Creek on the Bardstown road. The creek passes through part of his 1,200 acres. The house is set on a rocky knoll above the creek, is built of frame, slate roof, has hardwood floors throughout, hot-water heating apparatus, white Italian marble bathroom, and is furnished in the most luxurious manner. Cost $11,000.

Mrs. Ophelia N. Waggener's house on Highland avenue. Built in the Chateau style of red stone, St. Louis red brick with green slate roof. The house is built on a thirty-foot lot, but so well planned that the rooms are commodious. The mantels and furniture are of various hardwoods. Cost $8,000.

"Rio Vista," country place of Mr. J. H. Caperton, situated two miles east of the waterworks on an elevation about 400 feet above the river, has a commanding view of the city for miles around. The house is a frame structure. Although occupied by the Capertons but three of the summer months, it was built to withstand arctic weather. The walls and roof are made of three thicknesses and are padded with Cabot's quilting.

The house is equipped for a furnace, and is designed in the colonial style; the interior trim, fireplaces and furniture are in the same style, designed by the architect. Cost $11,000.

Left: M. Q. Wilson was the architect for Mrs. J. Moss Terry's residence at 1725 Third St., remodeled *ca.* 1899. *The Courier-Journal*, 28 January 1900. Below: The Paris H. Holzheimer House 1183 E. Broadway, was designed by Charles D. Meyer and erected *ca.* 1899. *The Courier-Journal*, 28 January 1900.

1325 Third St., 1961.

Residence of Mr. Thomas Keeley, 607 West St. Catherine street; built of Roman brick, with freestone trimmings; nine rooms. The ornaments on front are French Gothic. Cost $6,000.

Residence of Mrs. Minnie Laib, 1155 East Broadway; built of Akron, O., vitrified Roman brick; stone porch, slate roof. The stone carvings on the front are designed in the modern French Renaissance style. The interior is decorated and furnished in an artistic manner. Cost $8,000.

Dodd & Cobb have a number of most artistic houses to show for their architectural efforts during the past two years. Of these the beautiful residence of Mr. Samuel Grabfelder on Third avenue is perhaps the most elaborate. It is built of Rockcastle stone and is in a modified Italian Renaissance style. No expense was spared to make this dwelling, the stables and all accessories and detail most elegant. Messrs. Dodd & Cobb are also the architects of the dainty Whitney cottage, and the designers of the addition to Mr. Samuel Bush's house at Kenwood, in which is the Flemish library that has a well-deserved local reputation. In St. James Court, overlooking the park, is a pretty yellow brick house built by Mr. John A. Stark, and designed by the same architects. The most has been made of the view into Central Park, and the edifice harmonizes well with the quiet and retired. The house is well set off by its white limestone trimmings.

A new residence is that of C. C. Mengel, Jr., on Third avenue. It is of gray St. Louis pressed brick, Roman pattern, and the trimmings are of Bedford white stone. It is in the Italian Renaissance style, and a residence which has a beautiful effect from all points. John B. Hutchings was the architect.

The residence of Mrs. John A. Armstrong, on Third avenue, is after fine designs by Clark & Loomis. It is one of the most beautiful and original dwelling houses in the city. In a modified Renaissance style in design, but exact in detail, it excites admiration at once. The material is pressed brick, of Roman pattern, with Lake Superior red sandstone trimmings. The stone portion, with solid side-entrance steps, is a beautiful feature, also the symmetrical swells and double bays on the front. The

Above: Third St. north of Magnolia, 1903. The Samuel Grabfelder House is at left. Left: The Grabfelder House, 1442 Third St., was designed by W. J. Dodd and Arthur Cobb *ca.* 1899.

high-pitch roof gives a rather picturesque and not incongruous effect, which the alcove over the central window is an odd but acceptable trimming.

There are many other fine residences in progress of building in the city, indeed the foregoing is a short list. Enough has been given, however, to show the tendency of the hour and the strength of the present taste.

First in the Hearts of Her Citizens—Louisville's Homes

The Louisville Times, December 31, 1909

"There is magic in that little word—it is a mystic circle that surrounds comforts and virtues never known beyond its hallowed limits." Thus wrote Robert Southey of the word "home." The realization of its meaning is reached more fully here in Louisville than in any other city of the country, and that fact is widely known among the cities of the land. Those who come to Louisville from afar return whence they came with an abiding admiration for the instinct that teaches men and women of Louisville to make the home the paramount interest of their lives. Proportionately to its size Louisville owns more handsome and livable homes than any other city in this country; and the instinct is still fully alive.

From that time when Walnut street, between Floyd and Sixth streets, was the elegant residence district of Louisville, until the present time, the homes of Louisville have been noted for their beauty, their comfort and the gracious hospitality to be found therein. All changes in Louisville's conditions have been physical merely—the spirit has remained the same, whether homes have been made overlooking Cherokee Park, or out Third avenue, whether they have been made in Cherokee Drive, or along the lovely roads that make Anchorage the most beautiful village in the State. For Anchorage and other residential districts of similar character dot Jefferson county and are really a part of Louisville.

Louisville homes are in complete character. They are the havens to tired men, who find in them the repose and comfort made necessary by strenuous exertions in pursuit of the nimble dollar—for Louisville men, with negligible exceptions,

Above: "Elaborate Door-Knob Design," *The Courier-Journal*, 12 May 1889.

Opposite: DuPont Square with Fourth St. in background, 1897.

Walnut St. looking west from Fifth *ca.* 1890. Site of Founders Square and the former Armory at right.

are good workers, and make their work count. This accounts for the ability to make homes. Cares are laid aside and good friends gather. The latchstring, if the metaphor will carry, when the "latchstrings" are of carven bronze or polished brass or fine porcelain or cut glass, hangs ever on the outward side in Louisville, where folks use one another's homes with the same good will and enjoyment as they do their own. What is "home" to the Louisville man is home to his friend, and it is a poor degree of intimacy, indeed, that does not justify the casual dropping in to take a cigar or other refreshment in dining room, living room or library—or even in the pantry, if so be the family at home has elected to hold a session in that latter realm of food and drink.

At a time when Louisville was in the formative state, and the foundations of a great metropolis were being laid, the real spirit of the home was more considered than architectural fashions. Houses were built to live within, and some of the survivals of that day are not to be considered highly artistic, to say the least. But those are nearly all gone—the mansions of the old day. On the site of the old Shreve home there stands the First Regiment Armory—a monument to a farseeing Fiscal Court. The old house that gave way to this highly modern building was a landmark, and many of the older generation shook their heads sadly when it was dismantled. Other houses went with it, and Walnut street, although rather badly off, is daily taking on a more modern look.

The spirit of Louisville home life throve in many old mansions that have passed to make room for the encroachments of business, but for every one that has crumbled under the hands of the wreckers others have grown under the trowels of constructive artisans, and nothing has been lost. The shells of the departed day crumbled merely to release the spirit of the life of the home, and in its newer abodes the spirit lives to do credit to the men and women who established in Louisville a love of home and its concomitant virtues; and at the same time the fine and sweet hospitality that makes wanderers return to this great and hustling city for another taste of serene joys not to be found everywhere. The spread of population and an increase of architectural merit of late years has not marred, but has enlivened the love of the home that is traditional here.

While there was a decided Colonial tendency noticeable in the architecture of fifty years ago, between that time and the date of the birth of *The Times* there was a period of experiment with various and sundry applications of types of architecture that were no types at all. Not that there was any heavy loss in attractiveness—for Louisville homes have a charm all their own that radiates in spite of mixed architecture; but there was really nothing done in the building of homes that would particularly delight the ardent disciple of Ruskin. Even the boldest of our latter-day architects are unwilling at this time to put a name to some of the specimens to be found in the residential portions of the city. And yet those homes hold the eye from without, and hold the heart yet closer, from within.

When it was discovered a decade since that Third and Fourth avenues and their related thoroughfares would not contain the homes that must be built, the Longest farm bordering Cherokee Park came into prominence, and its once well-tilled acres are now the lovely grounds which surround handsome homes of well-to-do Louisville folk. No city of the United States can boast a more ornamental residence section than what is broadly termed The Highlands. Ten years ago—or a trifle more, perhaps—what is now variously known as East Broadway and New Broadway, was a very bad piece of road, and those residents who occupied the vast space upon which hundreds of handsome homes are now situated were known as confirmed lovers of the country. They are not extravagantly costly houses, but they are built—for the most part—upon defined and recognized lines of construction, and they are Louisville homes. That is of the main importance, after all.

Until ten years ago the lovely rolling hills surrounding Cherokee Park were bare of aught save trees and waving grasses. Nature is now highly adorned by the addition of numerous handsome residences—residences that justify the remark of a bright young woman, who, when she was recently asked where her place of residence was, responded, "I live above Cherokee Park; but not in the villa region."

Top: East side of Third St. south of Ormsby *ca.* 1910. The third and fifth houses from the left have been demolished. Bottom: Entrance hall of the Ferguson-Pearson House, 1912.

COURIER-JOURNAL
JOB ENG.

With all these changes and with the vast increase of the territory devoted to home building in Louisville there has been no change in the spirit of the home that has not been wrought by a plurality of bathrooms, electric lights, electric chafing dishes and the entrance of the motor car into the realm of domestic economy. We have more matters to fret over nowadays than we once had—that is, some of us have; but the more details to our homes the more joy to our friends and ourselves, and there it is. Nothing can rob Louisville of the distinction of being the real home center of the country. In Kentucky there were always homes—"always," in the sense of the word that recognizes the comparative youth of the section, beginning with Daniel Boone et al.—and Louisville learned what she knows from Kentucky. Anyone with full knowledge would admit that.

With the extension of the city's limits and the earning powers of some of Louisville's citizens, and the increase of unearned increment and the extension of normal usufructs, there naturally came to Louisville a desire to become somewhat of a town in the architectural line of business. Therefore the Italian Renaissance furnished some samples, and the people of Louisville, money in their pockets, got some Italian villas. Not because they wished to shame their neighbors who still lived in the nondescript mansions of another age, but because they believed in the home and wished to make it look good from the outside, so they might take more joy in entering thereinto, but also that their friends and neighbors might experience the same form of joy. There's nothing short about Louisville folks, to employ the language of the curb.

The villas were naturally for those of considerable wealth—those who could squander considerable money on a house, as one person expressed his thought. "Could squander" and "could afford" are terms that have a meaning other where that is widely different from their meaning in Louisville. To afford in Louisville when it comes to a matter of the home, means to do all that the circumstances will permit, depending, and with justification, upon a policy of good sense to cast the balance of fortune in favor of the homemaker. So, he who spoke of squandering in connection with the making of homes was

Above: South side of the 1100 block of East Broadway, 1903. All demolished except Mercy Academy at the east end.

Opposite: South side of Broadway west of Preston St. The house in the foreground was built by patent medicine tycoon John Bull, *ca.* 1871 and is now Turner Hall. The Isaac Wolf House next to it on the corner of Floyd St., built *ca.* 1865, is the site of the WAVE garden.

The Rev. Stuart Robinson's residence shown on the northeast corner of Fourth St. and Magnolia soon after construction (*ca.* 1872). Later owned by Mrs. Blakemore Wheeler, it was converted into offices by the Landward Company in the mid-1960s.

Opposite: Sketch of the Mission style Central Park shelter house by Alex Van Leshout, *ca.* 1920.

hopelessly in the minority, and doubtless he has so acknowledged by this time.

Then came the day of the Mission style, when the architecture of the old monks of Mexico was nicely imitated and adapted to the needs of this day and clime. They are scattered about through our residential districts, and they ornament those said districts. They look well, and they are Louisville homes. Whether Mission, Italian Renaissance or the ultra modern bungalow effect, the spirit of the Louisville home is there. Mission houses harbor the same warm hearts, the same cheerful happiness, and the same high regard for the home as do those done in the style of the unregretted Queen Anne—or the comely Colonial or the impressive Italian.

Bungalow, Italian villa, Mission style, or even those unlisted and unrecognizable forms mentioned, Louisville homes are all the same. They are homes and attractive ones. No city has so many that are beautiful in the proportion of its population as has Louisville. In no city is there so close attention paid, by all classes and orders of people to their homes. Investment in the home in Louisville is considered the very best of investment, dividends accruing daily and even hourly in the joy and peace that are obtained therefrom.

The stranger within our gates has ever remarked that Louisville homes far outclass those of other cities. Those who have enjoyed the privilege to enter many of them regard that privilege highly, and take good care that nothing may jeopardize it. Those who own them may realize the truth of these words, and those who do not, may doubt; but the Louisville home stands for itself, regardless of the spoken or written word—it is the Louisville home.

Illustration Sources

The Art Journal, Vol. 6, 1880 (Louisville Free Public Library), 100(2); *Art Work of Louisville, Kentucky*, Chicago, 1897 (The Filson Club), 7, 15 above, 37 below, 38, 53, 57(2), 58, 79, 81, 109, 114, 116, 144; *Art Work of Louisville, Ky.*, Chicago, 1903 (The Filson Club), 40(4), 80 above, 113, 143(2), 149; Joseph T. Barry Coll., 48, 65; *Catalogue of the First Exhibition*, American Institute of Architects, Louisville, 1912 (Louisville Free Public Library), 147 bottom; Louise Charlton Coll., 91 top; *The City of Louisville and a Glimpse of Kentucky*, Louisville, 1887 (The Filson Club), 104 left; *Commercial History of the State of Kentucky*, Louisville, 1899 (The Filson Club), 103 top; *The Courier-Journal* and *The Louisville Times* files, 20 right, 21 left, 59, 62, 75 left, 83 (Keen, 1955), 85, 91 bottom (Keen, 1954), 94 bottom, 105, 147 top; Mrs. R. Wells Covington Coll., 74, 87 left; Nancy Adams Drye Coll., Philadelphia, 92, 93 left; Ernest M. Ellison Coll., 23 below; The Filson Club, 24, 25 right, 26, 28, 34(3), 35(4), 37 left, 61 top, 66, 67, 112 bottom, 146, 151, (Frederick H. Verhoeff Coll.) 2, 8, 9, 11, 13, 18, 32, 39, 42, 43, 44, 45, 63(2), 101, 102, 103 bottom, 120, 121, 128, 129; William F. Furnish Coll., 49; Mrs. Norvin E. Green Coll., 5, 47, 51; *Harper's Weekly*, 4 August 1883 (The Filson Club), 110, 111; *Harper's Weekly Supplement*, 7 January 1888 (Louisville Free Public Library), 90, 139(2); James N. Keen Coll., dust jacket, 12, 15 left, 19, 54(6), 55, 56, 68, 72, 75 top and bottom, 78 above, 80 right, 82, 84, 99, 136, 137, 138, 142, 152; Lester S. Levy Coll., Pikesville Md., 29; Library of Congress, Prints and Photographs Division, front and back end papers, 22, 23 above, 27, 46, 97, 108, 115(2), 123; *Louisville Anzeiger* (The Filson Club), 33(2), 50, 148; Louisville Free Public Library, 106 above, 119; *Louisville Illustrated*, 1889 (The Filson Club), 64, 69, 70, 71, 73(2), 76, 77, 78 right, 88 above, 94 top, 95, 96 right, 98, 107, 131, 133; Mrs. Edward D. Morton Coll. 93 below; John C. Norman Coll., 60, 61 bottom, 150; Carter Ormsby Coll., 31; J. B. Speed Art Museum, 17; University of Louisville Photographic Archives, (R. G. Potter Coll.) 16, 25 above, 112 top, (Robin Cooper, Jr. Coll.) 104 above.

1510 Third St., 1961.